Supercat

Grace McHattie is a cat specialist, writing and broadcasting on all things feline. She has written five cat books, including one for children, and is a regular contributor to several cat magazines. Known as the cats' agony aunt, she advises on feline behavioural problems through her cat consultancy in Sussex, in magazines and on radio. She appears regularly on 'Going Live!', the BBC television children's series, and on many other television programmes. In 1987, she founded Adopt-a-Cat, a service which helps to bring together homeless cats and prospective owners. She has five cats of her own, including three jet-black moggies.

by the same author

The Cat Maintenance Manual
The Cat Maintenance Log Book
Problem Puss

SUPERCAT

The Non-pedigree Cat Care Book

Grace McHattie

Mandarin

A Mandarin Paperback
SUPERCAT

First published in Great Britain 1989
by Mandarin Paperbacks
Michelin House, 81 Fulham Road, London SW3 6RB
Text © 1989 Grace McHattie
Illustrations © 1989 John Mansbridge

Photoset by Rowland Phototypesetting Ltd,
Bury St Edmunds, Suffolk
Printed in Great Britain by
Cox and Wyman Ltd, Reading, Berks

British Library Cataloguing in Publication Data

McHattie, Grace
Supercat.
1.   Pets: Cats Care – Manuals
I. , Title
636. 8'083

ISBN 0-7493-0048-5

Contents

Cat Kit

Indoor or Outdoor Cat?

Feline Food

Contents

Moggy Miscellany

Moggy Maintenance

Moggy Medicine

Illustrations

Acknowledgements

I would like to thank the thousands of viewers of the BBC television programme 'Going Live!', who sent information about their cats for the fur survey, and Chris Bellinger and all of his team for making the survey possible.

Grateful thanks also to Dr Alan D. Walker for his help and expertise in checking the 'Nutrition for Cats' section of *Supercat* and Michele Conway for her invaluable comments on the 'Cat Colours' section.

Introduction

There are countless books aimed at the pedigree cat owner covering pedigree cat breeds, their care and their health needs. But – until now – no one has written a book about non-pedigree cats, which form the vast bulk of the cat population in every country in the world.

Their needs are just as important and they give their owners as much pleasure, yet these streetwise, hardy individuals usually only rate a passing mention in other cat care books, which may devote as much as a third of their pages to describing pedigree breeds. Although prettily illustrated, these pages are of little use or benefit to the majority of cat owners.

So I have devoted a book to the moggy, and to their own particular requirements.

It covers not only information such as their specialised care, diet and health, but tells you how you can turn moggy into mogastar. It explains why your cat looks like it does, helps with any problem pusses, lets you decide if you should keep your cat indoors, and will help the pensioner puss end its days in peace and comfort.

It explains why your cat (which is closer to nature than its pedigree cousins) behaves in the way it does and what its body language means. It tells you what to do when your cat goes missing, how to cope with pet loss, where to find another cat or kitten, and hundreds of other things you hadn't even realised you didn't know.

The moggy is the 'easy-care' cat, hardier than most pedigrees, more resistant to disease and more self-sufficient. Moggy kittens mature earlier than pedigree kittens, knowing most of what they need to know through instinct, and needing to be taught little by mother or owner.

In fact, the moggy is the cat with more street credibility. It deserves, in every respect, the title, *Supercat*.

Your Cat's Credentials

So what's in a name?

A lot – if you're a non-pedigree cat. Would you like to go around tagged a non-anything? Yet a search for a name more suited to the many positive qualities displayed by the moggy seems doomed to failure.

Strangely, no one knows for sure what the word moggy means. There is a great deal of argument about the origin of the word, which is used extensively in the United Kingdom but is virtually unknown elsewhere.

The people of the English county of Yorkshire, of course, claim it as their own invention. It's believed to be a corruption of the word mouse there. A cat is also a moggy because it is a mouser. In South Yorkshire, other words beginning with the letter M are frequently corrupted to moggy. Therefore, a pit moggy might refer either to a cat living at the top of a mine or to an actual miner.

As might be expected, the meaning in Lancashire is different. In most of that county, it means any cat, while in the western part of Lancashire it means a mouse.

In rural areas of England, country people refer to any small, furry creature as a moggy. Rabbits are known as moggies, as well as cats.

Inhabitants of the major port of Liverpool claim the name originated there in the eighteenth century. It's said that moggy is a corruption of margay, a species of South American jungle cat. Sailors were said to have brought them back from their trips and sold them to Liverpool warehouse owners to control the large rats the warehouses attracted. The margays were believed to have interbred with native domestic cats, producing striped tabbies.

A form of the word moggy may have been used in Shakespearean times. In *Macbeth*, one of the three witches says, 'I come, Graymalkin.' Graymalkin meant a grey cat and malkin could have been corrupted to moggy. Less attractively, the word malkin was also used to describe a sluttish woman.

Cats have often been identified with the unpleasant and there is a suggestion that the name may have come from the Old Norse word magi, meaning stomach, and used to describe any loathsome, stomach-turning creature!

Another Maggie who may have been responsible for the name was a music hall artiste of the 1890s called Maggie (or Moggie) Dowser. She was said to have always worn a fur tippet – her trademark. Legend doesn't divulge what this fur tippet had been when it was alive but it may have given its name to an entire section of the cat populace!

Another suggested corruption is that of mongrel to moggy.

However, the most likely originators of the word are those creative and colourful characters, those Londoners born within the sound of Bow bells – the Cockneys. The earliest printed reference to be found to the word moggy is by J. W. Horsely in 1911 in 'I Remember' where he attributes it to Cockney rhyming slang. It's probably as simple as 'cat and doggy . . .'

Readers of a cat magazine were asked to suggest a new name for the non-pedigree cat. Although the magazine had a circulation approaching 15,000, only one reader had an alternative suggestion – natural cat. A moggy is certainly naturally bred but the title is too much of a mouthful ever to find its way into general use.

So what else can they be called? At cat shows, non-pedigree entrants are referred to as household pets. Yet this conjures up a picture of a dependent creature whose only function is that of a 'pet'. The name just doesn't seem suitable for the free-ranging feline.

Even the title, domestic cat, doesn't really work. It doesn't properly distinguish the moggy from the pedigree, both of which are domestic cats as opposed to wild or feral cats.

Sometimes, cats of no particular breed are referred to as mongrels. That doesn't seem an entirely suitable name either. It is a name more usually associated with cross-bred dogs and has a growling harshness in its sound.

The title, non-pedigree cat, seems no better, having negative connotations. The moggy is not a *non*-pedigree; rather, the pedigree cat is a non-moggy, being bred originally from non-registered stock. All that 'pedigree' means is that the cat will breed true (have offspring which looks as it does) through four generations.

So we are left with the word moggy. Some owners don't like to refer to their cats as moggies as they feel it is a derogatory term, but it is a name I've always liked. I use it, as do many others, as a term of endearment and it's a word I will use often in this book to refer to our household, domestic, natural, non-pedigree Supercats.

What kind of cat have you?

A longhaired Calico – or – a mackerel tabby of foreign type. These cats sound much more interesting than 'just a moggy' but they are two of the many ways a moggy can be described.

Most moggy-owners don't know how to describe their cats at all. Many do not even appear to be sure whether their cat is a pedigree or non-pedigree. They can't describe their cat's colour, or markings, or distinguishing features.

The following section should help you classify your moggy. It should increase your knowledge of your own and others' cats and give you the means to describe your cat accurately should it ever become lost.

A cat is a pedigree only if it has a pedigree certificate – a piece of paper which gives the cat's name and breed and the names of its parents, grandparents and great-grandparents. So a cat should not be referred to as a Siamese (or a Persian) unless it has a pedigree certificate stating that that is what it is. It could be described as being of Siamese type – or foreign type (see 'Body type', p. 27). In the case of the 'Persian', it would be more correctly classified simply as longhaired.

Owning a moggy instead of a pedigree cat does not mean you are restricted as to colour, size, type or conformation. There are as many types of moggy as there are of carefully bred pedigree, so there is sure to be a moggy to appeal to everyone. And, of course, the same genetic rules apply to the make-up of any cat. Perhaps the knowledge of why your cat is a particular colour or shape or why its fur is a certain length will give it more importance in the eyes of others and destroy the 'just a moggy' syndrome forever!

Cat colours

Black cats
Your geographical location is likely to colour your opinion of the black cat. In the United Kingdom, black cats are considered to be very lucky and, should one cross your path, great good fortune is expected to follow. In the United States and Canada, black cats are considered *un*-lucky and white cats are the bringers of good fortune. In Ireland, folklore suggests that black cats have a magical ability to absorb pain and house cats, if black, are encour-

aged to stay in the sickroom so that the pain of their ill owners is absorbed.

What is certain is that black cats have been objects of mystery and fear for hundreds of years. During the witch-hunts they were often burnt at the stake with their owners as they were considered to be witches' familiars, or attendant spirits.

Did black cats receive their reputation as the embodiments of evil simply because of their colour? Black is often associated with evil, with the bad guys (just think of cowboy films and the bandits' black hats). Added to which, black cats will often have bright green eyes – another colour with sinister connotations.

Even today, charities which try to find homes for cats say that black cats are the most difficult to find homes for.

Black cats simply are not like other cats. They seem more independent than the rest of the species, already renowned for their independence, and often take longer to get to know. They seem to have 'shorter fuses'. Their feelings, sensitivities, likes and dislikes all seem to be very near the surface. They can be the most rewarding of cats if an owner is prepared to spend time and effort in understanding their pet, but they can be baffling to a less-involved owner or a stranger.

Possibly, this is the reason for the origin of their reputation as witches' familiars. Often, the people who were the objects of persecution were alone or lonely – the sort of people who would take the time, trouble and effort to get to know and understand their only friends – their cats. . . . Others, confronted by the aloofness, even unfriendliness, of that same black cat, might suspect some sort of mystical, magical relationship – when the truth was really much simpler.

Black kittens are often born with ghostly tabby

markings on their bodies. This is because the black cat is basically a 'double tabby'. Where a tabby has black stripes on a grey background, a black cat has black stripes on a black background!

Few cats are truly black. Even those who have escaped a white 'locket' usually have a few white guard hairs (strong hairs dispersed throughout the fur which protect softer parts of the coat). The true black moggy is a rarity. Even the true black pedigree cat is fairly rare as evidenced at cat shows where some owners can be seen tweezing out pale hairs!

Black and white cats seem to be quite different from their all-black brothers. The action of the white spotting genes appears to modify their personalities substantially, making them more outgoing, overtly friendly cats than their all-black counterparts.

Suggestions for black cat names: Abracadabra, Bovril, Cattandra, Cleopatra, Gandalf, Liquorice, Lucifer, Macaroon, Merlin, Midnight, Morgan, Pumpernickel, Taboo, Velvet.

Suggestions for black and white cat names: Ace, Beardsley, Boots, Domino, Felix, Galoshes, Garcon, Guinness, Korky, Mittens, Solitaire, Tuxedo.

Tabby cats
Tabbies could take over the world – at least, the world of cats. Every cat, even those which are all one colour (any colour), possesses tabby genes in its make-up. The agouti gene, which lets us 'see' the tabby pattern is dominant (a dominant characteristic is one which is always inherited directly from one of the parents), so it is thought that if all domestic cats were to interbreed, eventually mainly tabby kittens would be born.

Their name comes from Attabiy, part of old Baghdad, where watered silk was produced. The wavy pattern on the silk is very similar to the black stripes (or blue stripes) of the tabby cat.

In fact, the grey colour seen in tabbies is not grey at all. It is an optical illusion, formed by bands of black, brown and yellow colour, called 'agouti'. And, if you have ever wondered whether tabbies have pale stripes on a dark background or dark stripes on a pale background – it is the latter.

It is believed that the tabby originated when the small African wildcat, *Felis libyca* interbred with the striped Northern European wildcat, *Felis sylvestris*. Wild cats with tabby markings would have an edge over plain-coloured cats in the survival stakes as the broken pattern of stripes provides a perfect camouflage against foliage or rough ground.

There is more than one type of tabby marking. The familiar 'tiger' marking is that of the mackerel tabby with its bold stripes. Classic, or blotched, tabbies have heavier swirls of black along their sides with a mark shaped like a butterfly over the shoulder blades. Tabbies can also be spotted or ticked (there are bands of colour on each hair), but this is uncommon in the moggy. Many tabbies will have bracelets on their legs and rings around their tails and may have an 'M' on their foreheads which can make them look as if they are permanently frowning. Some moggy tabbies are a mixture of these patterns and they can have patches of white fur too.

Suggestions for tabby cat names: Bangles, Barnacle, Buttons, Chanterelle, Hoopla, Mushroom, Ninochka, Riff, Sarge, Tiger, Tiger Lily.

Ginger cats

So you think you've got a ginger cat? That depends on who you are talking to. A pedigree cat breeder will refer to a ginger cat as red and a geneticist will call the red factor yellow or orange.

Ginger cats are usually male but ginger females, although uncommon, are not rare. They occur only when the father is ginger or cream and the mother is ginger, cream or tortoiseshell. Uncommon though they are, I'm afraid they are *not* valuable in financial terms – much to the disappointment of excited owners who contact me from time to time under the impression that they have won the equivalent of a pussy football pools!

Some cats are such a pale ginger that they are really more of a beige colour – this would be referred to as cream by a pedigree owner. This is because the gene which arranges the colour pigment throughout the hair has mutated, causing the pigment to be dispersed in an irregular manner, and creating the optical illusion of a paler colour. Ginger cats which appear the true ginger colour have the hair pigment dispersed in a more consistent manner.

Ginger cats are really tabby cats underneath, hence the fact they are always striped. The gene involved acts like a coat of varnish, colouring the fur but letting you see the pattern below.

Ginger cats too, often show the effects of the white spotting genes in patches of white in their fur. As in other colours of cats, the white markings are first seen under the chin with small patches of white on their tummy. Cats with a larger degree of white will display white chins too and, where the gene has been particularly active, the cats will have white bellies and front paws. Back paws are 'next to go.' In fact, if you ever see an adult 'white' cat with one spot of ginger (or any other colour) on its back, it is not a white cat at all.

A coloured cat can be overlaid with the white spotting genes to an extreme extent which leaves it with one patch of colour – in other words, it is a coloured cat lurking under a white overcoat!

You may have noticed that a high proportion of cats used in television and film commercials are ginger. This isn't just because this colour is particularly photogenic, it's because animal trainers find ginger cats the easiest ones to train. They appear to have particularly amenable natures, are usually exceptionally friendly, intelligent and ready to have a go at anything for the right reward!

Suggestions for ginger cat names: Biscuit, Butterscotch, Cider, Fergie (Duchess), Finnan, Gingerbread, Keiller, Marmalade, Morris, Rufus, Rusty, Sherry.

White cats

All-white moggies are not very common and that may be just as well, as all-white cats can have problems peculiar to themselves.

One is deafness. Not all white cats are deaf but a significant proportion are. Some are deaf in one ear only. Contrary to rumour, cats need not have blue eyes to be deaf, although in odd-eyed cats (those with eyes of different colours) deafness may be found in one ear – the ear on the same side as the blue eye. Deafness is a side-effect of the gene which gives the all-white colour, and produces degenerative changes in the cochlea, the spiral passage of the inner ear.

Deaf cats can still make good pets but an owner should realise they will have special needs. It might be sensible to keep them as indoor cats from kittenhood, in order to protect them from predators and traffic. Otherwise, they can lead perfectly normal lives.

Vision may be a problem in those cats which are genuine pink-eyed albinos (rare in cats) or concealed albinos (that is, normal cats which have just one, inoperative albino gene but the ability to pass on albinism to their offspring). A new study by genetic researchers at the University of Utah has shown that these cats have an unusual pattern in the nerves linking their eyes and brains. The result of this is that affected cats have a distance perception problem. Cats (like humans) have binocular vision – they are able to judge distances because their two eyes see slightly different images and their brain converts this information into a perception of distance. Albinos and concealed albinos are able to see as if with only one eye, making hunting, for example, extremely difficult.

Some white kittens are born with one coloured patch, often on the back or shoulders, which disappears as the kitten matures. This mark is sometimes said to be God's fingerprint, left when He prods each kitten to see if it is 'ready'. Geneticists have not come up with a more logical explanation!

Summertime can pose particular problems for white cats, and for part-white cats. The skin underneath white cats' fur contains no pigment, being a delicate pink in colour. It is similar to the skin of a natural blonde human and needs similar protection. Although fur protects most of the body, the ear tips do not have much of a fur covering and are prone to sunburn or even skin cancer. To protect them, white cats' ears should be covered, on sunny days, with zinc and castor oil ointment, or a preparation recommended by a vet.

Suggestions for white cat names: Bacardi, Bianca, Blanche, Buttermilk, Cassata, Dumpling, Marshmallow, Smirnoff, Snowdrop, Snowflake, Tang, Yuki.

Tortoiseshell cats
Tortoiseshell cats are nearly always female. They are also referred to as Torties and are brindled ginger and black in colour.

Females have two of the chromosomes on which the orange gene can travel while males have only one. The female then can have one gene for orange and one for non-orange, which means that the orange gene can colour part of her coat but the non-orange gene will allow other colours 'underneath' to show through.

So tortoiseshell males are rare: they have some curiosity value but are of no particular financial value. It is thought most tortoiseshell males are infertile.

Some tortoiseshell cats' markings are almost mirror images. They can have lines down the middle of their faces, one side of which will be black while the other side is ginger. The introduction of the white spotting gene alters the tortoiseshell patterning drastically. The pattern, from being brindled, becomes patched. Tortoiseshell and white cats are referred to by the elegant name of Calico in the USA.

Tortoiseshell and white cats can be ginger, black and white in patches, or cream, blue and white in patches. Rarely, a cat of one colour has ginger patches or blue patches with no white.

Tortoiseshell and Calico cats are usually dainty, feminine and delightful company – real ladies, in fact.

Suggestions for tortoiseshell cat names: Caraway, Cinnamon, Chrysanthemum, Gingersnap, Goulash, Pastiche, Tamale, Tortilla, Treacle, Truffles.

Suggestions for tortoiseshell and white cat names: Calico, Chutney, Harlequin, Jumble, Medley, Mosaic, Pansy, Patches, Pickles, Popcorn, Pierrot.

Blue cats
A blue cat is really a grey cat which is really a black cat.

Actually, blue is the word used by pedigree cat owners to describe the colour most people would call grey. The same gene mutation, called dilution, which makes some ginger cats look very pale in colour is at work in scattering and reflecting black pigmentation so that we see it as blue.

Blue cats, like black cats, have grey skin under their fur, while paler coloured cats have pink skin underneath.

Not many moggies are blue, as the gene for dense colouration is dominant over the dilute gene.

Suggestions for blue cat names: Angel, Bluebell, Bumper, Gordon (Bleu), Lancelot, Picasso, Sacre Bleu, Shadow, Sixpence, Smokey.

Longhair or shorthair
It is not only coat colour which varies from cat to cat – coat length does too. Shorthair is much more common than longhair, which accounts for only 14 per cent of the United Kingdom's moggy population.

Owners often refer to 'fluffy' cats, meaning that they are longhaired. These cats will usually go through several changes of coat, from their relatively shorthaired first coat at birth, to a fluffier kitten coat at around six months, to a heavier adult coat at twelve months or later.

Longhair can be 'carried' by a shorthaired cat, so two shorthaired cats can produce a longhaired kitten. However, shorthair cannot be carried so two longhaired cats will always have longhaired kittens, even if their own parents were shorthaired.

Both long and shorthair have their advantages in moggy society. Longhair provides a greater degree of protection and warmth for outdoor cats but shorthair is more easily cared for by the cat itself. The benefits appear to average out because the life expectancies of longhairs and shorthairs are roughly equal.

Although no one appears to have done a study on the subject, observation leads me to surmise that cats sharing a common coat colour may smell more alike (to another cat) than a cat of a different coat colour. Introducing a new cat into a household could be easier if it is a similar colour to a cat already living there!

Eye colour

Most cats have eyes of green, yellow, ranging through to gold, or, most rarely, blue. Black moggies will almost always have green eyes in comparison to their black pedigree brothers who must have yellow eyes. White cats will sometimes be odd-eyed; they will have one yellow eye and one which is green or blue.

Body type

There are three body types in the cat world: cobby, moderate and foreign.

The cobby cat has a chunky body with sturdy legs and a broad chest. The head is also short and broad, usually with wide-set ears.

Most moggies are of moderate body type: well-proportioned with a slim, muscular body, legs of medium length and a head of good proportions.

The foreign-type cat is one which usually has some pedigree ancestry, with Burmese, Siamese or another type of foreign pedigree cat in its background. These cats are slender, long-legged and elegant, with slim, often wedge-shaped faces and large ears. Due to their ancestry they are often very noisy!

Fur colour distribution

Tabbies are still outnumbered in the United Kingdom by seven to one – despite the fact that the tabby patterning is dominant to all non-tabby colours.

Black and white cats – and black cats – are the top cats, making up two in five of the United Kingdom's cat population.

NORTHERN IRELAND

SCOTLAND

WALES

	Black & white		Ginger
	Tabby		Tortoiseshell & white
	Black		No overall predominant colour

*Predominant cat colours
throughout the United Kingdom*

Information on the colours of moggies, and their distribution, was sadly lacking until the young viewers of BBC television's 'Going Live!' programme helped me put together a picture of the nation's cats by sending me details about their own cats. Over 2,000 viewers responded and the information in this section was gathered from that survey.

It has always been assumed that the various colours of cats are evenly distributed throughout the country, but this would seem to be incorrect.

Tabby cats have numerical supremacy in Avon and Northern Ireland, as well as Sussex, where the various colours appear to be distributed more evenly than anywhere else.

Ginger cats come out tops in Essex, Herefordshire and Warwickshire, and tie for first place with black and white cats in Middlesex.

Wales has a particularly high proportion of tortoiseshell, and ginger and white cats, and Kent shows a high proportion of blue, and tortoiseshell cats.

It would be interesting to speculate on the effect of living on a small island on colour distribution but too few respondents from the United Kingdom's islands took part in the survey to come to a valid conclusion. However, the Channel Islands did show a majority of the less-common colours – tortoiseshell and white, blue, and blue and white. The Isle of Wight, too, had as many white cats as black and white cats, and the same number again of ginger and ginger and white cats.

9 counties had more black cats than any other colour, and 29 counties and areas out of 49 had more black and white cats than any other colour.

The most commonly occurring colours, in order, are black and white, black, tabby, ginger, tortoiseshell, ginger and white, tortoiseshell and white, tabby and white, white, blue, and blue and white.

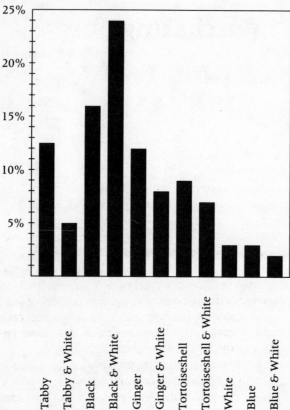

Cat colours in the United Kingdom

Purchasing Puss

Why do you want a cat anyway?

Several years ago, a survey in the United States revealed that 60 per cent of people ignore their cats most of the time. 10 per cent have cats as status symbols and 30 per cent say that they keep cats for companionship.

As moggies aren't usually kept as status symbols, you must be one of the 90 per cent – and, hopefully, one of the 30 per cent! Because you never get the best from a cat if you ignore it.

They are not the solitary creatures of popular legend. They live, for choice, in social groups. If a cat lives with a human, that human becomes part of the cat's social group and the human becomes the chief cat in the household. As such you have certain duties: you are the provider of food and a comfortable and secure place to sleep, the cat's protector, the maker of the house rules and, *more importantly*, the provider of love and companionship.

A cat will only put into its relationship with you as much as it gets out of it. Ignore the cat and it will begin to ignore you, looking on you only as a provider of food and comfort. So those who insist that cats are self-serving and egotistical are saying much more about themselves than they are about their felines. For example, what sort of impression do you get about the *owner* of this cat described in a Dorset newspaper: 'Eccentric home wanted for aggressively unsocial ginger tom (neutered). Answers to the name of Misery Guts.'!

Cats are a responsibility and ownership of one should never be entered into lightly. (Those who say that cats cannot be owned cannot be fulfilling their role as chief cat adequately.) Do think carefully before giving a home to a cat. It will probably be with you for around eighteen years, during which time it will cost you around £4,000 to £5,000 at today's prices.

Treat your cat well and you will find that is the best investment you will ever make.

Pet stores

Never buy a kitten from a pet store.

For the majority of people, buying a kitten means buying from the local pet store but usually this is the worst possible place to buy.

Despite the fact that there are many excellent pet shops, run by caring and considerate staff, the make-up of the cat is such that it simply is not a suitable 'product line' to buy from a shop. The better pet shop owners have acknowledged this fact by refusing to 'stock' them.

However, in the summer months when kittens literally cannot be given away, some uncaring owners who have not had their cats spayed dump box-loads of kittens on pet store doorsteps. The pet store staff often will not take the kittens to an animal charity for fear they will be euthanised (it's often an incorrect assumption) so they take them in and sell them to recover their costs in caring for them.

Cats and kittens are susceptible to many diseases and ailments which can be passed from one to another in the confines of a store. These can range from an easily dealt with problem such as fleas to a life-threatening respiratory disease which can then be passed on to any other cats you own.

If you buy a kitten from a pet store, you will not be able to meet the kitten's mother or, usually, learn anything about her. You will not know if she is strong and healthy or – more likely – if she is a poor, worn-out, underfed cat allowed to become pregnant again and again because of an owner's uncaring attitude, or for the sake of the small amount of money gained in selling her kittens.

Ear mites and fleas will be the least of the problems you will be buying. You can almost guarantee that the mother cat was not wormed at the correct time and the kittens will consequently be full of these parasites. The kittens will probably be barely weaned and may be far too young to have left their mother. Six weeks is an absolute minimum age for an exceptionally well-developed, well-nourished and healthy kitten to leave its mother and eight weeks is better. (Most pedigree kittens do not leave their mothers until they are twelve weeks old.)

Kittens from different litters and different households should never be placed together because of the risk of cross-infection, but litters are sometimes mixed in pet stores. The conditions in which the kittens are kept are far from ideal in other areas too. A small wire cage with no heating, no privacy and frequently no fresh water, either is guaranteed to put a young kitten under stress which will make it more susceptible to illness and disease.

Many animal organisations strongly advise that kittens should not be bought from pet stores and some are campaigning to make it illegal to sell a cat or kitten in a store.

So don't buy your kitten from a pet store. If we all refuse to buy kittens from this source the shops will cease trying to sell them.

Unfortunately, some stores carry on because kind-hearted customers buy kittens because they feel sorry for them or because they are obviously ill. Although their motives are laudable, they are helping keep these pet store owners in business. So if you see kittens which are too young for sale, or are obviously ill or badly kept, complain to the pet store owner if you feel brave enough, then complain to your local council who must license and control pet stores. If you feel there is cruelty of any kind involved, contact your local animal prevention of cruelty charity too.

Friends' cats

Every summer, friends have unwanted kittens to give away. They will become even firmer friends when you say that you will take one of them.

Apart from making your friend eternally grateful, this is one of the better ways of acquiring a kitten. You may already have met the mother cat and will know if she is healthy and has a suitable temperament. You can ask your friend if the kittens have been wormed or inoculated and you can arrange to take your kitten away at a suitable age.

The kittens' father may also be known. According to research carried out at the Universities of Cambridge and Zurich, it is the father's temperament which will be passed on to the kittens; the mother's personality has no effect at all! I don't believe it, but anyway, it does no harm to discover if dad is a paragon among pusses or a moggy monster.

Rescue centres

You may be surprised to learn that rescue centres are probably the best places to acquire a cat or kitten.

Don't expect them to be mangy old strays; you will find the fittest, healthiest, most beautiful animals there.

The moggy breeding season is January to September, so many pregnant mums are abandoned by their owners from February to October, rescued, if lucky, and give birth between March and October. It follows that kittens are abundantly available from May onwards, tailing off around December.

Rescue centres are consequently overfull with kittens needing homes from May to the end of the year. They would not be overfull if people wishing to acquire a cat or kitten sought them out, for the animals are an excellent 'buy', having been well cared for by experts (usually volunteers), inoculated, even neutered (if old enough). The shelter volunteers are only too willing to give advice to any new, unsure owner and the cost of the cat or kitten is negotiable – usually a donation.

Some even have special OAP schemes – they will help match up an Old Age Pensioner cat with an Old Age Pensioner person. A few will even guarantee the new owner that the rescue centre will pay all veterinary bills for the cat's lifetime – giving an older person on a limited income peace of mind and a companion for their golden years.

Rescue centres don't encourage impulse buys – they know that most kittens bought on impulse end up back at the shelter – so usually no cat or kitten is handed over on the day it is chosen. In most cases a volunteer will visit the offered home before handing over the animal, simply to ensure that a good home is being offered and that the new 'owner' is not adding to their income by supplying the needs of vivisectionists.

Although some of the larger rescue organisations will euthanise cats and kittens if homes are not found in a specified time, most of the smaller centres will never put down a healthy animal. They are therefore always over-full, giving a prospective owner a good choice of animals.

So do search out your nearest rescue centre. Some are quite large and well-organised and can be found in the telephone directory; others are small – perhaps run by just one person – and can be tracked down via local vets, pet shops or cat lovers.

Advertisements

It doesn't always pay to advertise.

You may see kittens or cats advertised in your local paper, shop window or veterinary surgery. The success of these advertisements depends on the time of year. In mid-summer kittens cannot be given away.

It's a buyer's market, so choose carefully. The vet's noticeboard is a good place to start looking because the surgery staff should know something about the mother cat – and you should be sure to ask them.

Wherever the kitten is advertised, do ask to see the mother cat as well as the kittens. If she looks worn out, unhealthy or ill, don't buy one of her kittens. The odds are that they too will be unhealthy and you'll end up paying large veterinary bills . . . and it could end in heart-ache if your new kitten dies.

Do you really want a kitten?

Most people, when deciding they would like a feline companion, don't consider whether or not they really want a kitten. Often, a full-grown cat would make a better pet, especially for the elderly or for young children.

Kittens are more active and more likely to cause accidental damage and injury; more expensive in the long run – they will have to be inoculated and neutered; more time-consuming – they will need company and will have to be trained in the rules of your home.

You also do not know quite how a kitten will grow up. When it loses that first fluffy cuteness, you might wish you had considered an adult cat instead! Adult cats do take longer to settle in a new home than kittens but there are many other advantages to consider, such as less expense if the cat is already neutered.

Often, an elderly person would like to have a cat for

companionship but they worry that the cat will outlast them and become homeless. This is an ideal situation for an adult cat, maybe even an elderly cat, from a rescue centre. The cat gets a home; the elderly person gets companionship.

Male or female?

Frankly, it doesn't matter at all.

Some people swear that male cats are more friendly, some say that females are more affectionate. Both are correct – sometimes. There is not any real difference in terms of how good a pet the cat will make.

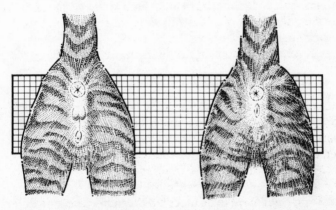

The only slight difference will come when you have your cat neutered (you *will* be having your cat neutered, won't you?). For a male cat (above left), the operation is less major and consequently slightly cheaper.

Nobody's perfect

I have met many cats which are handsome, loving and with a delightful disposition – yet they have spent five or ten years in a rescue centre and will probably never be offered alternative homes. The reason is that they have some sort of physical imperfection – a missing eye or ear or leg.

Although you should ensure that any cat or kitten you buy is *healthy*, this is not the same as being physically perfect. It's amazing how well a cat can cope with just one eye or three legs and it is something the owner comes not to notice after a while. So, if you do come across a cat which needs a home and it has some sort of disability, don't immediately reject it. If it has a personality you like, it could be just the cat for you.

When a cat is disabled, its other senses compensate. Deaf cats can lead very full lives, but should be kept away from all traffic and unfriendly dogs, as they cannot hear their approach.

Blind cats remember where furniture and food bowls are placed and find their way around by feel. Some completely blind cats can still catch birds!

Of the many thousands of cats I have met, two particularly stick in my mind. One was a gorgeous ginger cat called Jasper, who, as soon as he met me, put his arms round my neck, hugged me and purred like a steam train. He had only one eye because he had been used as target practice. He had spent half a dozen years in a shelter and had no hope of a home because of his missing eye, yet he was one of the nicest cats I have ever met.

The other nicest cat I have ever met was the winner of a competition I organised to find 'The Tattiest Tomcat'. McGee had been a stray involved in an accident and had lost a leg – which did not slow him down any. Most people didn't even notice that he had only three legs. He won the contest because of his charm and personality and appeared on breakfast television with Miss World. I'm pleased to say that all the technical crew and presenters ignored Miss World and made a great deal of fuss over the lovely McGee!

When a cat chooses you

Chances are that the sad-eyed stray on your doorstep is a confirmed scrounger who could give Meryl Streep a few acting lessons.

Some cats which already have good homes are experts at scrounging extra meals from kindhearted neighbours. Some are so clever that they have a night-time home with their owners and another, daytime home with neighbours who also believe themselves to be the cat's owners!

So, before you take a 'stray' cat into your home, you should make every effort to discover if it really is a stray. Ask friends and neighbours if they know the cat but don't rely on that – the craftiest cats will ensure their second homes are at some distance from their first homes. Buy an elasticated cat collar and attach a message holder, complete with message, to it. Enclose your telephone number and ask the cat's owner to contact you. If the message is not removed and you do not hear from any other owner, you should then inform local rescue centres and vets that you have the cat, as well as advertising it in your local newspaper and in shop windows.

Somewhere, some child or elderly person may be missing their only companion, so it is well worth making the effort. If the cat turns out to be genuinely lost, take a few health precautions before introducing it to any other cats you might have (see 'Introductions' p. 45 later in this chapter).

Cats are property in law and a previous owner has six years in which to claim back their cat. That has to be a consideration before you or your family become fond of a stray cat.

In truth, and contrary to popular belief, it is very, very rare for a cat to stray. It is much more likely to have been abandoned or become lost.

Those which have been homeless for some time may have become so used to an outdoor life, or so wary of humans that they may come to you for food but sleep elsewhere – perhaps in a garden shed or greenhouse. They should be allowed to stay out of doors if they wish as they will become frightened if forced inside. Over a period of time they may come to trust you enough to come indoors – but this could take years.

Choosing

There's no such thing as a free lunch or a free kitten.

If buying a kitten, ask to see its mother and try to gauge her state of health. If she is ill or run-down, her kitten will be too, although that may not yet be apparent. Don't take it, even if it is free. It will probably cost you a lot of money in veterinary fees and maybe a lot of heartache too.

Is the cat or kitten coming from a clean home and one where it appears to have been looked after well? Incidentally, a smelly home is not necessarily a bad home. If large numbers of cats are kept together, some of them will spray their urine around the home in order to establish and mark their territory.

Pick up the cat or kitten and look at its fur. It should be clean with no matts or tangles. Part the fur and look for fleas; there should be no black specks of flea dirt. Check for these around the ears, under the chin and by the mouth and around the top of the tail.

Backbone and hipbones should be well-covered with flesh and there should be a solid, weighty feel to the kitten. It should not have a pot belly.

Lift the tail and check that there are no signs of diarrhoea. The anal area should be clean.

Look in the kitten's mouth. Teeth should be white and gums a healthy pink. Red gums are inflamed and pale gums may be a sign of anaemia.

Next, have a good sniff! The kitten should not have bad breath, and its ears should have no smell. The ears should look clean inside with no dark wax present. If the kitten is shaking its head or scratching at its ears there may be some infection present.

Eyes should be bright and clear and the third eyelid should not be visible across the inside corners of the eyes. If the kitten has weepy eyes, *do not* buy it, whatever the reason given by the vendor – it may have a respiratory disease which could be passed on to any other cats you might have.

Is the kitten weaned? It should be *at least* six weeks old and eating solid food before leaving its mother.

Of course, you might go to look at a kitten which turns out to be very obviously unwell and you feel so sorry for it you take it home just to ensure it receives veterinary treatment. If you do so, be prepared for large – and continuing – veterinary bills. Kittens which have a poor

The third eyelid

start in life are often sickly throughout their lives, having never had a chance to build up resistance to infection. And there is a very good chance that the kitten will not survive the first few months.

Also, if you already have a cat at home, you must strictly quarantine the newcomer or you run the risk of exposing your cat to infection. This means keeping them apart in separate rooms, preferably two rooms separated by a corridor or another room so if your new kitten is sneezing it will not spray contaminated droplets over your cat. It also means 'scrubbing up' thoroughly each time you have handled the kitten and before touching your cat. Disease can be transmitted so easily by contact that you should change your outer clothing and wash and disinfect your hands and arms each time you go near the kitten.

If you have come across a kitten for sale which is obviously ill and the vendor is not prepared to seek veterinary attention, report the matter to your local animal cruelty organisation.

The trip home

If you give as much thought to taking your new pet home as you have to choosing it, you will not be sharing a car with an escaped tiger in miniature which gets stuck under the pedals and then throws up on the back seat.

You may have chosen your kitten several days or weeks before you are able to take it home and this will give you time to provide the equipment it will need, including something to take it home in.

You'll need a cat carrier many times during your cat's lifetime – every time you visit the vet (which should be at least once a year), to take your cat to a holiday cattery, or to a cat show, or when you move house. So it's sensible to make a good investment the very first time you need a carrier. Your new kitten will be lively, and probably a little frightened by its first taste of the outdoors, so a secure carrier will make moving it much easier.

There are many different types of carrier. The cheapest is a cardboard carrier with handles and ventilation holes. Like the cardboard box it resembles, it is only really suitable in an emergency. A cat cannot see out of the box and may, in fear, start ripping it to shreds to try to escape.

Wickerwork carriers with plastic-coated wire fronts are popular. These look quite pretty and have the advantage of giving your cat some privacy while enabling it to see where it is going. Some of these carriers also double as cat beds. The disadvantages are that, if the carrier is used at different times for more than one cat, it is almost impossible to clean or disinfect between times; cats love sharpening their claws on wicker; and it can easily snag your stockings or trousers!

The best cat carriers are made of plastic-covered wire and are plain, rectangular, with a carrying handle and a fastening latch which slots into a loop. They can be slightly more expensive than the other types but will last a lifetime. They are easily washed and disinfected. If you ever visit a cat show, these carriers are often on sale and usually at a price a little less than you would pay elsewhere.

Some carriers combine a plastic-coated wire front with a plastic or glass fibre body. Although these give the cat privacy and are easily cleaned, they are not quite as strong as the all-wire carrier and will not last as long. The latest type, of moulded resin with a mesh front, has castors on the base and a foldaway handle, allowing owners to tow their cats along behind them.

It is much easier to remove a reluctant cat from a top-opening carrier than a side-opening one.

When you go to collect your new kitten, leave your carrier open on the floor where the kitten can jump in and

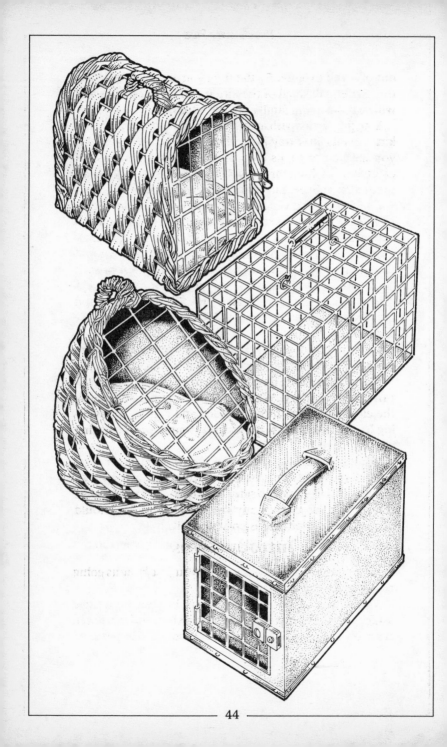

out of it and explore. By the time you are ready to leave, the carrier will smell of the kitten and its littermates and will be much more familiar to the kitten.

Line the carrier with an old warm blanket and place the kitten on its litter tray for one last time before leaving! If you have far to go, its probably best if the kitten has not eaten for an hour or two. Travelling, especially in an unfamiliar vehicle, can make a kitten carsick.

Check with the vendor what type of food your kitten has been eating. Ensure you have some of this at home as eating a familiar diet will minimise the risk of tummy upsets. You needn't necessarily believe it if you are told the kitten will only eat bread and gravy – this means that it is all the owner has bothered to give it. But always introduce a new diet gradually – give the kitten bread and gravy along with the properly balanced diet you have chosen for a day or two.

If you have not already done so, before leaving ask the vendor if the kitten has been wormed or inoculated.

It is less unsettling for the kitten to be transported, in its carrier, by car or taxi. Walking, with the kitten buffeted by the elements, is not recommended and neither is travelling by bus, with all its noises and strange people staring into the carrier.

Whoever is driving should be asked to drive smoothly and not too fast, taking corners carefully so that the kitten is not tossed from side to side. The kitten may well protest throughout the journey anyway, but the journey should be made as comfortable as possible for it.

Introductions

Perhaps you already have a cat and you just *know* its going to adore your new kitten. Wrong!

Your cat or cats occupy a position in your household which they have carved out for themselves and this kitten is simply a usurper who is going to threaten that position.

So don't expect them to welcome it with open paws . . . they'll have to beat it up first!

They will do this to establish their dominance over the kitten. Fortunately, most kittens are easy-going little fellows who do not want to be top of the heap anyway (that comes later) so the ear-cuffing, spitting and hissing usually doesn't last too long if a kitten is being introduced— as long as you do it the right way.

Introductions really start before you go to collect the new kitten. It really is a good idea to quarantine your new kitten for a few days, even if you are convinced it is completely healthy. Sometimes an illness can be developing and the symptoms may not be apparent for a few days. If you are in the slightest doubt about your kitten's health, you *must* quarantine it (see p. 42). Quarantine also has another benefit. It allows cat and kitten to become used to one another's smells before they actually meet.

When the meeting is to take place, trim their claws (see p. 169). There will be some fighting but they will do less damage to one another.

Then have a stiff drink. If you feel relaxed about the introduction, your cats will be less uptight.

Have your cat on your lap and stroke it in its favourite places. Tell it what a clever cat it is and how much you like (love) it. If you can ask a friend to bring in the new kitten, that is ideal; however it is done, *you must not be seen to be making friends with the kitten until your cat has made friends with it.*

There should be plenty of furniture in the room, affording hiding places for the kitten, if necessary. Alternatively, you can spread some large cardboard boxes around the room which will serve the same function.

Your friend can sit down with the kitten on his or her lap. The cat will immediately jump down and go over to sniff the newcomer and the kitten, if bold, will jump down and sniff back. Some hissing, spitting, chasing and boxing round the ears will ensue and you will probably start feeling very sorry for the kitten.

Don't interfere – this has to be gone through for the kitten to learn its position in the new society it has found itself in. The noises made can be quite bloodcurdling and can go on for hours, frightening many owners into intervening. This is not necessary unless the kitten is really being hurt. I have never known a cat really hurt a newly weaned kitten; it is just showing it who is boss. . . . And kittens are pretty clever anyway: when they have had enough they will find somewhere to hide.

The worst of the fighting should be over on the first day (and you could be lucky and find the two do not fight at all) and only minor skirmishes may ensue from then on.

Some cats and kittens settle down together almost immediately. Others take more time; it could take up to a month for each to completely accept the other. With older cats it can take much longer; introducing an adult cat to another adult can lead to arguments for a year or more, until they get used to one another.

Dogs and cats can settle down well together if introductions are carried out in the same way described above, with the dog under control (wearing a leash if necessary) and being told very firmly that it must not chase the cat. Puppies and kittens get on very well: if they grow up together, it is usually the cat which becomes 'top dog'.

I don't think it is a good idea to introduce cats or kittens to most small prey animals which are also kept as pets. Some cats do have white rats as best friends but it does seem unfair to keep them together. Remember that rabbits are rodents. Although we may think they're cute, a cat is unable to distinguish between a rabbit and a rat and many owners have come home to find their pet bunny with its paws in the air and their cat looking pleased with itself. Although some cats do make friends with pet rabbits, a cat cannot be blamed for attacking what would, in the wild, be food.

Some cats never do settle down together completely. Cats, just like people, can be incompatible. It isn't too surprising when you think that a cat is suddenly expected to share its food, its people, and its bed with a stranger . . . and they haven't even been properly introduced!

Your new kitten's first day

If you already have a cat, your new kitten will probably think it has arrived in Alcatraz!

Its first day or two may well be spent closed away in the bathroom or kitchen while they get used to one another's scent, until you can ensure that the kitten isn't harbouring any illness. If this is the case, remember that your kitten will be feeling lonely. It has just left a warm and comforting mother and three or four littermates, with whom it has spent the last month or so playing and learning how to be a cat.

So spend time with your kitten, whether or not it is in 'quarantine'. It will want to explore at first, so ensure there is nothing left around which can harm it. Put away breakables such as ornaments because, although adult cats can pick their way along a crowded mantelpiece without dislodging anything, your kitten is more like a toddler – blundering around with much less control over its movements and co-ordination.

If you have open fires, place fireguards over them. Fireplaces (when the fire is unlit) should be blocked off. It is not a good start in a new home when a sooty kitten has to be rescued from the chimney.

Supply your kitten with its own feeding bowl, which should be separated from any other feeding bowl by at least 2 to 2½ metres – strange cats don't like eating close together. Feed your kitten four small meals a day, until it is three or four months old (its tummy is very small), then it can be fed three meals a day until six months, with at least two meals daily thereafter. A vitamin supplement should be added to its food until at least six months of age.

Play with your kitten; it will take its mind off the strange surroundings and will help form a bond with you. However, don't play with it to the point of exhaustion. Adult cats will sleep sixteen hours a day and kittens will sleep longer than that, so have plenty of rest breaks. If there are children in the household, make sure they understand the new 'baby's' need for sleep.

Let it have somewhere warm and comfortable to sleep; a place it can call its own, even if it is only a cardboard box. Let that be the kitten's sanctuary and do not disturb it while it is there.

For the first few nights, place a warm hot water bottle under its blanket to simulate the warmth it would have received from its littermates. A ticking clock will comfort it with a reminder of its mother's heartbeat and an old stuffed toy will give it something to cuddle up to.

This is the time for you to decide where you want your kitten to sleep. If you let it sleep on your bed the first night it will expect to cuddle up to you for the next eighteen years or so. A Gallup poll showed that 34 per cent of women allow their pets to sleep on their beds and 18 per cent of all cats sleep on their owners' beds. So make your mind up and use ear plugs if the kitten's plaintive miaows from the kitchen are bothering you.

It isn't particularly hygienic to share a bed with a cat and its occasional little passengers but many people like to have their cat in bed with them – it gives them a sense of security. A cat is an early warning signal of danger. At the first hint, off it goes!

Cat Conduct

Early days

Psychologists say that a child will be shaped for the rest of its life by its experiences up to the age of five years. The same is true of the first six weeks of a kitten's life.

If, during those first few weeks, a kitten becomes used to gentle handling by humans, it will become human-orientated and will live happily with humans for the rest of its life. If, during the first few weeks, it has contact only with other cats, it will become a snarling, fighting spitfire when it first meets a human and may never become 'tame' enough to live as part of a household.

By the age of six weeks, some moggies are mature enough to leave their mothers; their personalities, their reactions to humans and other cats are already indelibly set.

New-born kittens are like blank slates; they are creatures waiting to learn – they cannot see, hear or walk. Their eyes, always a deep blue to start with, don't open for a week or more. Often, one eye will open before the other, giving the kitten a raffish look. (Eyes should be left to open at their own rate; never force open a kitten's eyelids.)

Newborn kittens can squirm around on their bellies, using their legs to propel themselves, rather like oars, well enough to reach their mother's teats. Usually, each kitten will have its 'own' teat so there is no squabbling at feeding times. Mother cats will start purring as soon as their kittens are born and the sound helps the kitten find its mother; its sense of smell helps it home in on the one teat it will use.

Kittens knead either side of the teat with both paws, using a rhythmic, regular movement, to express the milk. As kittens are born with a full set of claws, this must be fairly painful for their mother.

The pleasure of feeding from its mother is one memory which a cat will carry throughout its life. The kneading movement becomes associated in the kitten's mind with a very pleasurable and satisfying experience and, in adult life, when it is happy it will repeat these kneading movements with its paws to express happiness. This is why many cats knead their owners' laps before settling down, much to the owners' discomfiture. There is nothing you can do about a kneading cat; kneading is too deeply ingrained as an instinct for remonstration to be effective. All you can do is keep your cat's claws trimmed.

When kittens have finished their feed, their mother will clean them. Cats are extremely clean creatures but some are cleaner than others. The mothers which do the most washing of their kittens are those who were washed most often by their own mothers. Those with careless mums tend to be a bit *laissez-faire* themselves.

A cat will clean her kittens from top to bottom – literally. This is to stimulate excretion of waste products which she will also lick up. That might sound pretty disgusting but it has high survival value. In the wild, the cat's nest would have to be kept spotlessly clean and sweet-smelling so as not to attract any predators to the location. The mother herself will excrete well away from the nest but, as she will not want to leave her kittens too often at first, she will become a model of continence. She may not relieve herself for several days and this is frequently echoed by the domestic cat who may not urinate or defaecate for several days after giving birth.

Anyone who is left with the responsibility of hand-rearing very young kittens should realise that they will not only have to feed the kittens every two hours but also rub their tummies gently after every feed to stimulate excretion.

So licking becomes associated in a kitten's mind from the earliest days with being cleaned, cared for and looked after by a doting mum. Licking for the adult cat then, is not just a means of keeping clean, but a source of relaxation which exerts a calming effect.

Getting licked

Have you ever noticed your cat trying to jump from one piece of furniture to another, falling, then sitting down to give itself a few hard licks?

Owners put their cat's expression and behaviour down to embarrassment because the cat has failed in a task. In fact, the cat has probably frightened itself a little and licks itself in an attempt to calm down.

Another reason for this washing may be to clean away the scent of any sweat. Cats only sweat through their paw pads and they perspire when frightened. By licking their paws to clean off any sweat it is less likely that a predator would be able to find them or follow them.

Because one of a cat's earliest memories is of its mother licking it, licking becomes a symbol of dominance. When two cats settle down to have a nap together, one will often lick the other. Owners think this is a cute sign of affection but really one cat is telling the other that it is the boss.

Cats' mums care for them in ways other than licking them. Young kittens are completely dependent on their mothers for the first six weeks of life and their mothers live up to this responsibility. Cats are extremely good mothers as a general rule but can also be strict disciplinarians when necessary.

As kittens mature, like all children everywhere, they come to dislike being washed. They will wriggle and squirm, trying to get away from their mother and her insistent tongue. To stop them wriggling, the cat will gently grip her kittens around the neck using her teeth. The kitten will immediately go limp. This is a protective device; should the kitten be grasped by the neck by a predator, it would play dead. As many predators, including the cat, are attracted by movement, a seemingly dead kitten might be of less interest.

This is also the source of the behaviour noticed by many worried owners when, during boisterous play, cats or kittens close their teeth around one another's necks. A cat will also grasp another cat around the neck to show dominance over it. Usually, this is not done with enough pressure to hurt. It is a controlling device as the other combatant is expected to go limp – and usually does, whereupon it receives a vigorous washing from the victor. (Sometimes a cat will grasp its owner's wrist in this way to demonstrate that the owner is doing something the cat wishes the owner would not do.)

Be good – or I'll bite your whiskers off!

Another, less usual way a mother cat has to 'discipline' her kittens is to bite their whiskers off!

A kitten, just like a cat, uses its whiskers as a sort of antennae, which helps it measure distance and interpret information from its surroundings. If a kitten is boisterous or obstreperous, chewed whiskers will slow it down considerably!

It is at this time that cats prove, if proof were needed,

that they are not the solitary, sly, self-serving creatures of popular legend.

Female cats are extremely supportive towards one another during the birth of kittens and afterwards. They will help one another give birth, the more experienced among them acting as midwives, assisting inexperienced mothers by cutting umbilical cords, opening birth sacs and licking kittens clean.

After the kittens are born, cats will suckle other cats' kittens – if they are allowed to. Many mothers are very protective of their kittens and will immediately 'rescue' any which have been taken for feeding by another cat.

Female cats will also kitten-sit for one another. This would enable a cat which lived wild some time off for hunting, without leaving her kittens defenceless if a predator found the nest.

With supportive assistance like this, it is hardly surprising that cats are such successful survivors, even when left to their own devices.

Killing and cannibalism

The first few weeks in a kitten's life are when it is most in danger of its life. It is at risk from strange male cats – and its mother.

A first-time mother may not recognise her newly-born offspring for what it is. A new-born kitten is somewhat rat-like in looks and mewls plaintively immediately after birth; this can frighten an inexperienced mother.

If the kitten finds its way to, or is placed at, her teats, the mothering instinct takes over as the kitten starts to suckle. If the instinct is not triggered in time, the mother may kill and eat her offspring, believing it to be a prey animal.

The first few weeks are crucial. Female cats need to remain undisturbed in order to nourish their kittens. In the wild, they would have prepared a cosy nest, hidden from view and safe from predators, in which to raise their kittens. In the home situation, owners should try to duplicate these conditions as much as possible.

Cats find a nest of their own, if their owner does not provide one. Usually this is under the bed or in an airing cupboard but one cat in Derbyshire, said to be very timid, gave birth to her kittens 4½ metres up a tree, in an abandoned magpie's nest!

If a new mother is disturbed, either by humans wanting to look at the new kittens, or other animals intruding, the cat may decide to move her kittens. This she does by holding them in her teeth and carrying them to a new location. (Although a cat will carry kittens by the scruff of their neck, this is obviously the only option open to her and should not be copied by owners, as carriage in this way places a great strain on the kittens' neck muscles.) Some mothers, however, are frightened of carrying their kittens – they become upset at the kittens' squeals. Some of these mothers will start carrying around surrogates instead; fluffy toys or dolls. Owners should be on the alert for this behaviour because it means the mother feels insecure about her kittens and wants to move them.

Occasionally, a cat will feel so disturbed and worried about the safety of her very young kittens that she will kill and eat them. Horrifying as this might seem to us, this behaviour does have survival value. If the mother thinks the young kittens are in danger she knows they are helpless and have little chance of surviving. So nothing is 'lost' if she kills them, because she thinks they will die anyway. However, much is gained. By eating them, she is absorbing high-quality protein which makes her stronger and better able to give birth to further litters of kittens.

In nature, nothing is wasted.

Young kittens are at risk from strange tomcats too.

Owners of a cat which has just kittened should ensure that there is no way that full (un-neutered) tomcats can gain access to the house. This means keeping cat-flaps and windows closed at all times.

If a full tomcat gains access to the kittens, he will kill them. Cats, like all living creatures, are on earth to perpetuate their race by passing on their genes to the next generation. If a tomcat kills kittens, the mother will come into season again more quickly; giving him the opportunity to impregnate her, thereby passing on his genes in her kittens.

Cats – the perfect predators

It has been said that, if a computer was given the requirements for a perfect predator, it would come up with a cat.

Cats have forelimbs which move in all directions, allowing them to twist and turn rapidly in pursuit of prey. Their hind legs are large in comparison to their forelimbs, and have great muscular strength allowing them to spring and leap at their target.

Most cats, including the big cats, have claws which retract into sheaths when not being used. Cats hone their claws to needle-sharpness on suitable surfaces, such as trees, and then retract them into their sheaths, to prevent them being blunted by contact with the ground.

Adult cats have 30 teeth: 12 incisors, 4 canines, 10 pre-molars and 4 molars. Kittens develop milk teeth at around one month which are shed during the following months until they have a complete set of adult teeth at around six months. The incisors act like scissors, shearing meat into pieces. The pre-molars and molars are used for gnawing bones. The cat's rough tongue is perfectly designed to rasp meat from bones. Cats are also helped in their hunting by their whiskers which help them gauge width and, some believe, are bent downwards when hunting at night to guide them over rough ground. Their hearing gauges directional location extremely well.

But what makes the cat such a good hunter is its eyes. Without moving its head, a cat can see more than a semi-circle; about 180–190 degrees. Because its eyes are situated at the front of its head, the field of vision of each eye overlaps the other by about 44 degrees. This enables a cat to judge distance very accurately and, by swaying its head, it can further pinpoint distance.

The cat's eye is about four times larger proportionately than the human eye. The whites of a cat's eyes are barely noticeable as the coloured iris is proportionately huge. The cat's eye is more curved, with a deeper-set lens, than a human eye, which gives a cat a view at least five times brighter than any human can see. Nerve cells called *rods*, which respond to light, occur in a ratio of approximately 25 to 1 to *cones*, which respond to colour. In humans, the ratio is 4 to 1. This, coupled with a sensitive pupil which enlarges from a vertical slit to a circle to permit more light to enter the eye when light is limited, makes the cat a perfect nocturnal predator. Cats *do* have colour vision in normal light conditions but, in limited light, only the rods are active and cats become colour blind. In the dark, all cats *are* grey – to another cat.

Hunting – are cats cruel?

When a cat catches a prey animal, only to let it go again and then recapture it, it is being no more cruel than a human athlete competing in a race.

Kittens will begin to play at around the age of one month. Their play involves pouncing on their mother's tail, which she will wave from side to side to attract them.

This is the first stage in learning to hunt; springing on to a moving object.

Cats are attracted to their prey by movement; they have specific brain cells which respond to the tiniest amount. Their eyesight is not good, close to, and a cat will often not be able to find a treat placed directly under its nose. A moving target is quite different and a cat will have no trouble in seeing it. Movement triggers the hunting instinct in a cat.

Cats living wild will bring back small, dead, prey animals for their kittens to practise on. The animal will be tossed around by the kittens who will bat it with their paws. In this way they learn the feel and smell of a prey animal. Later, when the mother cat feels her kittens are old enough to cope, she will bring live prey back to the nest for her kittens to catch and kill.

Prey animals can pose a threat to a cat; a bite from a rat or even a mouse can cause poisonous abscesses to form on a cat living wild, which may eventually kill it. Therefore, the prey must be subdued so that it poses no danger to the cat. A cat, if unable to deliver a killing bite immediately, will hit it on the head with its paws. This causes the prey animal to lower its head and in this position it is unable to bite back at the cat.

Sometimes, if the cat is unable to kill the animal, it will hook the prey with its claws and toss it in the air. This is designed to stun and disorientate the animal – it is not a form of play. The cat will continue to manoeuvre the animal until it is in a position to kill it with a single bite to the back of the neck.

The cat may continue to toss the prey animal around after it is dead and this, too, is seen as 'play' by owners. But it is not. Just as a trained athlete has to become 'psyched up' to compete in a race with adrenalin flowing and senses fine-tuned, a cat has to be psyched up to make a kill as it often poses danger to the cat too. An athlete cannot finish a race and immediately go and read a book; a calming-down period is necessary and the same is true of a cat.

If it is any consolation, it is believed that an animal which is killed by another feels little or no pain. As it is bitten, endorphins (hormones which are natural pain-killers) attach to the surfaces of cells responsible for pain perception, and the prey animal does not suffer.

Playing cat and mouse

You can tell the difference between a pretty little bird and a vicious rat, but your cat cannot. This was demonstrated recently in the Scilly Isles when two hundred bird-watchers arrived from all over the country to watch an American grey-cheeked thrush which rarely visits the United Kingdom. As they watched, a ginger tom called Muffin ate it.

A cat cannot modify its behaviour to suit the type of prey it is chasing. A rat can kill a cat so, to be a successful survivor, a cat has to treat all prey animals as rats.

Playing cat and mouse is an expression in everyday usage, taken from the behaviour of a cat which will catch its prey, and let it go, only to catch it again. Again, this is not play. Because the cat's hunting instinct is triggered by movement, if it catches an animal which then plays dead, the cat may become confused and lose interest, only to have its interest revived immediately the animal starts moving again.

Cats will hunt anything small which moves. You have often seen them hunting dressing-gown belts trailing on the floor. In the wild, cats will obtain their nourishment from a variety of prey, including insects – and indoor cats will often be seen stalking a fly with as much care as their wild cousins will devote to a rat or rabbit. This will not do them any harm, will give them good exercise and will probably make them feel good too in performing an instinctive behaviour pattern.

A survey in the *Journal of Zoology* of 80 cats in an English village revealed that they caught and brought home more than 1,000 prey animals in a year, despite the fact that 6 of the cats caught nothing at all. One cat caught 95 animals and woodmice and sparrows were the most common catch. Three times more prey was caught between June and September than between December and March.

There is a country saying that May kittens make poor cats and this may be attributed to the fact that the mouse population is at its lowest ebb in May. Therefore mousing females in kitten would not be so well nourished as they would be later in the year.

Cats which are kept as mousers should be fed a good diet too; it has been proved that cats hunt better when well-fed than when half-starved. Males and females make equally good mousers.

Cats which don't hunt probably had mothers which didn't hunt either and so didn't pass on their expertise. There are exceptions to this; there does appear to be a race memory of hunting which enables some cats with no experience to become accomplished hunters.

If a cat brings its catch home, it is often thought to be contributing to the group's food stores. Some cats will line up their catches on the doorstep and some will lay them neatly in their feeding bowls. Some cats, however, are simply looking for a quiet place to eat or keep their catch until they are ready to eat it and will growl warningly if you try to take the prey from them.

Although some prey food can probably be eaten with beneficial effects (birds, for example, will be eaten feathers and all, providing valuable roughage) other prey food is dangerous; for example, rodents which may be poisoned or carrying tapeworm cysts.

Take these away from your cat – if it will allow you – and bury them in the garden where they can nourish your plants. If your cat brings home an animal which is still alive, it may give it up if you provide something else for it to chase – a trailed string or rolled ball. Rescue the animal and place it in a box containing soft lining in a quiet place while you telephone your vet for advice. Your vet will often be able to put you in touch with organisations which rescue injured animals or birds.

Incidentally, although cats will catch voles, they won't eat them. They taste bitter!

Putting a bell on your cat will not always prevent it from catching birds and animals, because of the way cats stalk their prey. They will approach cautiously, pausing in between, until they are close enough for a spring from behind any available cover. They are very patient and will wait behind their ambush until the creature is within striking distance. Hunted like this, a bell is unable to warn a bird of impending danger.

At least one owner has stopped her cat's hunting exploits by giving it a good talking-to. She explained that it made her miserable and the birds were not too thrilled either. From being a real menace to birds, this pussycat stopped hunting them entirely and even gently brought home a robin with a broken leg for attention!

Cats don't have it all their own way when hunting, however. If they eat too many grasshoppers, they'll suffer a severe case of constipation! Cats love to hunt the wriggling slow-worm, which looks like a snake but is really a lizard. When caught by the tail, the slow-worm will break it off (it can grow another) and then wriggles off in two directions at once. The expression on a cat's face at this feat is a picture to behold!

The social cat

Kittens learn to fight early as preparation for the world, when they will fight to protect their territory and to win females within that territory.

Kittens will start the rough and tumble with littermates at the age of four weeks or so. They will chase one another, leap out from ambushes and have semi-serious fights.

The kittens who are best at fighting soon find that the best position is underneath and they will roll on their backs, waving their paws and inviting attack. In this position, the kitten has five sets of weapons free; its four sets of claws and its teeth. It will grasp or smack with its front paws, while biting (usually on a tender ear) and raking with its back paws on its opponent's tummy. The kitten on top can only bite when it manages to dodge the other kitten's paws and only has one paw free itself to fight with as it is standing on the other three!

When cats live wild, even cats which have once been pets, they join together in groups. These groups have a better chance of survival as any danger noticed by one cat will immediately be transmitted to all.

Living wild, in a feral group, there will always be a chief cat. It is always an unneutered male, although not necessarily the largest male. This cat will fight to preserve his status and keep his 'own' females. These fights are very noisy but involve a great deal of ritual, enabling protagonists to back off at any stage if unsure of their chance of success. During fights, the most serious injuries are usually torn ears and scratches. Although the cats have the ability to injure one another severely this rarely happens as they simply want to demonstrate who is boss. Having done so, the fight ceases, although the victor might mount the loser in simulation of copulation, to demonstrate its superiority.

Fights also occur over a female in season and tomcats will congregate from many miles away to pay court. (This is why unneutered house cats disappear for days at a time, often coming back injured, even if there are no unspayed females living nearby.) Fighting will take place, not so much for the female's favours, but for the territory on which she lives. The female will make her own choice of mate and this will not necessarily be the winning cat. In fact, the likelihood is that she will be mated by several of the males.

As female cats ovulate in response to mating they may ovulate for each one of a number of matings and consequently produce a litter of kittens which all have different fathers.

Status symbols

The female hierarchy of a feral group is linked to the number of litters she has produced; a fertile female holding a higher position than one who has had fewer litters. Cats which have been spayed or neutered will hold a lower position in the hierarchy. In a household of neutered cats, the most dominant cat could well be a female, especially if she has ever had a litter of kittens.

Feral groups of cats often live in the environs of institutions, such as hospitals, where they eventually become a nuisance as they grow in numbers, with an unpleasant (to humans) smell of their sprayed urine in their territory. In some cases, the reaction of the building's owners has been to have the cats poisoned. More recently, welfare groups have trapped the cats, neutered them all and, after cutting a tiny slice from the tip of the ear to show that neutering has been carried out, have re-released them into the wild. Some of these welfare groups are now reappraising this procedure, as neutering of the cats alters their standing within the social group.

The higher the status of a cat in the group, the more food it will get as it will eat before the less-dominant cats, and the more comfortable its living conditions will be. In return, the more dominant cats will protect the less-dominant from outside dangers. Cats are very supportive towards one another and a call of distress from one will result in the other group members rushing to its aid. Cats will help an injured cat, even if it is a stranger to them. One owner heard a cat miaowing outside her door which led her up the garden to where her own cat was lying injured under a hedge.

Less-dominant cats will try to find sleeping places which are high up, which gives them a good view all around and makes them feel more secure.

When cats live with a human owner, the hierarchy still exists, the main difference being that the owner will take over the position of chief cat, with the responsibilities which come with it. Affection will be readily shown by a cat to its owner when the owner shoulders this responsibility in the hierarchy. Many owners are afraid of being boss as they fear they will lose their cat's love. The opposite is true. An owner who gives up their responsibilities as chief cat will confuse their pet, who may even react aggressively towards their owner to keep the owner in line as the *cat* is chief cat.

Each cat has its own way of showing affection, and its own time. A few cats may lead fairly independent lives all day but snuggle up on an owner's lap in the quiet half hour before bedtime. One cat living in a multi-cat household may only show affection when the other cats are not present. Give your cat the opportunity to show affection and you might be surprised at just how friendly it is. Stroke your cat in all its favourite places (under the chin, behind the ears) when it comes to you for a cuddle.

Some cats expect their owners to show affection in odd ways. A few like nothing better than being gently slapped on the bottom by their people!

Territory

Neutered cats have much smaller territories than un-neutered cats. They are not usually dependent on their territories to provide their food.

Food, however, is what territorial behaviour is all about. In the wild, the size of territory available to a cat is closely linked to the amount of food available to it in the form of prey.

Cats are very territorial and will strongly resent inter-lopers. A house cat, in an urban area, will undoubtedly have to lay claim to its own garden, which will already be 'owned' by another cat. This is why cats, when they first move house, are usually loath to go out of doors at first.

However, in many densely-populated areas, cats' territories will overlap. Each cat will consider its own garden – and those on either side if another cat does not live there – as its own and will defend it from other cats. Towards the edges of its territorial boundaries, other cats will be tolerated as the outer fringes of their territories overlap.

Cats patrol their territories along clearly defined, unchanging paths and can become quite upset if, for example, an obstacle is placed along one of 'their' walls. As they patrol, they mark their territory in ways which other cats will recognise.

They will scratch tree-trunks, scent from the glands on their paws marking the trees with their own particular smell. Most upsetting to neighbours, they will spray their urine (and both males and females spray) on vertical surfaces as a scent marker. Or they will urinate or de-faecate in gardens they consider their own. Very assertive cats will not cover up their waste products, so the scent remains much stronger. These are all ways of marking territory with smell. Cats will renew these markers regularly as the scent lessens with time or is washed away. It is believed that cats know not only which cat owns a piece of territory by the smell, but also how long it has been since the cat visited it, by the strength of the remaining smell.

Arguments over territory will occur when cats come face to face on their territory pathways. There will be a ritualistic hiss, and an aggressive stance will be taken, after which one of the cats is expected to move away, usually back the way it came. If it does not, a fight may ensue.

Territorial pathways may explain the myth of the cat who walks alone. Although social and sociable creatures, the cat does like to take its own path and share it with no one!

How do you make friends with a cat?

It's easy – don't look at it!

In the cat world, a stare is threatening behaviour. So if you stare at a cat, it thinks you are threatening it. This is why cats always go to people who do not like them – because someone who dislikes cats does not look at them and the cats feel unthreatened and secure. (When told that they can prevent cats from coming to them simply by staring at them, few cat-haters take the advice – secretly they're rather proud that the cat has singled them out!)

So if you'd like to make friends with a strange cat, don't look at it, and get down to its level. A cat can be intimidated by a huge human looming over it, so lie on the floor, not directly facing it. Do not stare at it and make no sudden movements or noises. Blink slowly at the cat and, every so often, give a silent yawn. If the cat is extremely nervous, turn your back on it! This technique works because it uses cat body language to communicate to the cat your friendly intentions.

A cat which wants to show its dominance over another cat will stare fixedly at it, contemplating attack. Often, a confrontation can be avoided if you place an obstacle in the cats' line of sight. If they cannot see one another, they often will not bother to fight at all.

A cat which wants to prove to another that it is no threat will blink frequently, sometimes lifting its head and looking down its nose to do so. It has been said that blinking slowly at your cat is the feline equivalent of giving it a kiss. If the cat closes its eyes in response, the kiss is returned.

The size of a cat's pupils is an indication of its mood. When the pupils enlarge, the cat has become alert. Half-closed eyes are a sign of contentment.

The least threatening gesture a cat can make is to turn its back on another cat (or human). In this position, it is impossible for it to fight and few cats will attack a cat whose back is turned to them.

Yawning is another sign of reassurance in the cat world and can also be used by humans to show friendly intentions. It is not only our domestic cats which recognise these signs; the big cats too will respond to them. However, before yawning at a lion or tiger, ensure there is a strong fence between you!

How can you tell what your cat is feeling?

Watch its tail, ears and whiskers – and listen to it. A happy cat will carry its head and ears high and its tail will stick straight up in the air. A very happy cat will curve its tail towards its back. A slowly wagging tail will show that a cat is alert and a wildly thrashing tail will show it is angry.

Ears are an excellent indicator of a cat's mood. Upright ears mean it is alert and happy and ears swivelled to the side show extreme happiness. Ears are flattened as soon as a fight is imminent; this protects delicate eartips from injury as fighting cats always slash at one another's ears with their claws.

Whiskers move into different positions in response to mood. A cat about to fight will draw its whiskers back to emphasise the snarl. When a cat anticipates something pleasurable, such as food, it will draw its whiskers forward.

An anxious cat will twitch its ears and lick its lips rapidly. A worried or nervous cat will 'flehm'. It will begin to gasp and inhale air through its open mouth. The mouth contains the Jacobson's organ which allows a cat to taste and smell at the same time and the worried cat is using this organ in this instance to taste and smell danger.

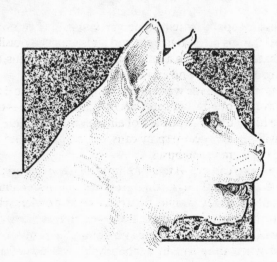

A welcoming cat will bounce up against its owner, tail and head held high. It is trying to reach the owner's face, to rub faces in cat greeting. Cats have scent glands on their chins and lips, so by rubbing its face and chin against you, it is covering you with its scent and letting other cats know that you belong to it.

A cat also has anal scent glands so, if after rubbing its face against you it turns around, you can only assume you are being invited to have a sniff! Cats greeting one another after an absence will sniff one another's faces, then sniff one another's bottoms.

If a face is proferred, you can sniff back but don't blow, as a cat will take that as an unfriendly act; a silent hiss.

Why do cats hate to be laughed at?

For years it has been thought that cats hate to be laughed at because they are sensitive souls. I have a much more sensible interpretation: they think you are hissing at them.

What happens when someone laughs? The mouth opens, the lips are drawn back and air is expelled noisily.

What happens when a cat hisses? The mouth opens, the lips are drawn back and air is expelled noisily.

Cats use the hiss to warn of their intentions and to deter the advance of another cat. Cats hate not only the sound of the hiss, but the expulsion of air which accompanies it, and will run away from spray cans, bicycle pumps and the noise of air brakes on buses.

Some cats can growl too – for just the same reason that dogs do. I once thought that growling was a hereditary trait only, as many families of cats are great growlers while other cats never growl at all. However, it does seem that cats which come from non-growling families can learn to growl when they live in a household of accomplished growlers!

How do cats purr?

The purr of the cat has been considered so mysterious that it was once thought the cat possessed a 'purr-box' in its throat.

Dr Lea Stogdale and Dr John Delack solved the mystery in 1985 in *The Compendium of Continuing Education for the Practising Veterinarian*.

They state that purring has a dual origin, the result of alternating activity of the muscles controlling the larynx and diaphragm. This causes a change in air pressure which creates vibration which makes the sound of the purr.

First, the shape of the 'voice box' is changed by narrowing the glottal opening which causes the air pressure to increase. The vocal cords are opened up and the pressure is released while the glottis remains open, allowing the cat to breathe. The release of pressure causes vibration in the respiratory system which results in the sound we call the purr.

The purr then involves not just the throat area but the diaphragm, as can be demonstrated by lightly feeling your cat's throat and ribs when it is purring.

Purring displays different degrees of pleasure: the rougher the purr, the happier your cat is feeling. However, if a cat has suffered a respiratory illness such as cat 'flu, the purr may always sound rough and rasping.

A mother cat will begin to purr as soon as she gives birth. This serves as a directional signal to her kittens who are then able to find her and her milk.

The purr is not always a sign of comfort. An anxious cat will purr from nerves and a sick cat will often purr as a sign it is in pain.

A German fairy tale gives the definitive reason for the cats' purr.

A princess had to spin 10,000 hanks of thread within a

month to save her handsome prince from death. She knew she would never finish her task in time so she asked her cats to help her. They all worked without cease and finished spinning the thread just in time to save her prince. The cats were rewarded for all time by the gift of the purr – the noise made by a whirring spinning wheel.

What do cats dream of?

Cats probably dream of many of the same things we do: comfort, love, food, friends – and enemies, pursuit, and fear. For cats, just like us, can have nightmares too.

As much as 60 per cent of cats' sleeping time is spent dreaming. Humans will dream for only about 20 per cent of their sleeping time.

When cats (and humans) dream, their eyes move beneath their closed eyelids. This is called Rapid Eye Movement (REM) sleep. During REM sleep, pulse and breathing rates vary and brain activity becomes similar to that of the brain in its waking state.

Cats will often make sucking motions with their mouths while asleep, undoubtedly dreaming of their first pleasurable experiences, and some will dribble while asleep. At other times, they can be seen with twitching legs and faces, obviously disturbed, and trying to run away from a dream enemy. If your cat is having a nightmare, gently waken it by stroking it and talking to it quietly.

Do you ever dream about cats? According to dream interpretation, if you chase it away, you can overcome all obstacles to achieve fame and fortune. A miaowing cat signifies that a false friend is secretly causing you harm. Dreaming of a white cat means a setback in finances and a black cat means a windfall. If a woman dreams of holding a cat her conduct will be the subject of speculation!

Cat Kit

Because pet stores are limited, usually by lack of space, in the amount of cat accessories they can carry, many owners do not realise that there is an extremely wide range of equipment available. If your local pet store is not able to supply you with whatever you require, you can find advertisements by manufacturers and mail order suppliers in cat magazines.

However, do fill in your own name, not your cat's, if ordering by mail. One owner in the United States used his cat's name, Tiger Ann, so his cat began to receive a lot of unsolicited mail – even a letter from Ronald Reagan, who was President at the time, inviting her to join his Victory Fund! (She joined.)

Cat beds

And so to bed

Legend has it that cats are ornery critters so it follows that a cat will always choose to sleep on the best armchair, the fluffiest rug or some favourite but inaccessible place, even when a comfortable alternative is provided.

This theory can be laid to rest. Modern cat beds are so well-designed, comfortable and appealing to cats that they are used in preference to other sleeping places. There is such a wide choice available that you should give some thought to your cat's preferences and the type of home you live in before purchasing.

If you live in a chilly, older-style property, a hooded bed

might be your first choice. These are sometimes called 'igloos' and have raised sides with a hooded top. This type of bed will cut down considerably on the draughts which every self-respecting cat does its utmost to avoid. Cats unused to this type of bed can be wary of it, taking several days to adjust. In households of more than one cat, the hooded bed is often used by one of the cats to ambush the others, making them slightly uneasy about approaching it!

A similar type of bed is high-sided and will keep out draughts without hiding the cat from view.

There are many variations on these designs and the modern ones are completely machine-washable. This is important where cat beds are concerned as fleas will use beds and blankets as breeding areas. The beds are foam-filled and covered with a variety of fabrics, including fur fabric, and some manufacturers will cover beds using your own fabric, so your cat's bed will fit in with the rest of your colour scheme. The size of the bed is very important, so don't be tempted to buy a kitten-size bed at first – your kitten will probably outgrow it. Some cats like to sleep curled up, so a small bed would suit them, whereas other cats sleep stretched out and would not fit comfortably in a small bed. Your cat's own body temperature and the location of the bed will affect the size of bed needed; when a cat is cold it will sleep curled up, stretching out as it warms up.

Until you get to know your kitten's preferences, it's probably best to provide a sturdy cardboard box as a sleeping place. Keep the sides high, just cutting down part of one side for access and place a clean old blanket or towel in the bottom for bedding. A few newspapers could be placed under the blanket for additional warmth. The box should be thrown away after a month or two and replaced with a new one. Blankets should be shaken out and washed regularly to remove fleas and loose fur.

A type of bed which is rapidly finding favour is the beanbag. Cats enjoy scooping a hollow in the bags which then mould around their bodies, conducting heat around them. Beanbags for pets are filled with polystyrene fire-retardant beads, an important point when choosing a bed for a cat, most of whom like to sleep near a fire. Some beanbags sold for human use are not fire-retardant; however, even fire-retardant materials should be used sensibly. Fire-retardant means just that and should not be confused with fire-proof.

One big advantage with beanbags is that they will not harbour fleas at all. Beanbag covers zip off for washing and the filling can also be washed in its inner bag. It should be given a good shake and the bag hung up to dry, preferably in the sun.

One disadvantage with beanbags is that they confuse some cats completely. They are filled with polystyrene beads, which sound just like cat litter underfoot. So owners, who have been told that cats never soil their own beds, are mystified when they find that their cat has soiled their beanbag. Most cats get the hang of it after a while, though.

Other bedding accessories are available for cats. If your cat already has a favourite, but not very luxurious, bed, or prefers a cardboard box, there are fleecy blankets which can be placed inside for extra warmth. Real sheepskin pet blankets are available as are fleecy blankets in man-made fabrics, which are washable.

Pets have their own electric blankets too. Small vinyl pads and metal panels are available which run on as little as 10 watts of electricity, so are very inexpensive to use. They are particularly effective for keeping older cats and young kittens warm. Flex protectors are also available for those cats which chew wires.

If, after all that, your cat still will not use its bed, try

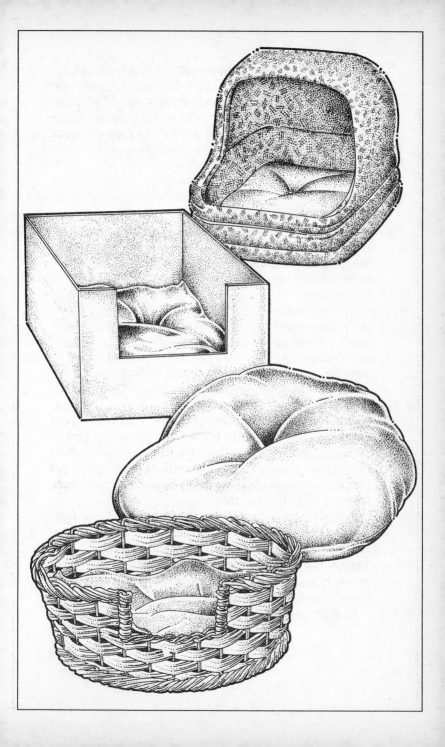

changing its location. Cats prefer to be in a warm situation, away from draughts and in an area where there is not a lot of through traffic. Some cats, especially those of a nervous disposition, like to sleep high up, as they would do if they were living wild. Place their bed on top of a wardrobe or kitchen cupboard and they will enjoy the high life.

Cat litter

Litter-ally speaking

Cat litter is a fascinating product yet is taken so much for granted that most people don't even know what it is. For example, did you know that it was a tried and tested antidote for Paraquat poisoning?

Although many cat owners in the United States, with its higher proportion of indoor cats, purchase cat litter regularly, only around 40 per cent of cat owners in the United Kingdom supply it for their cat's constant use. Often, an owner will buy cat litter for a new kitten to use during the first few weeks in its new home but will then make a determined effort to train the kitten to 'go' outdoors. Cat litter should really be supplied to every cat, indoor and outdoor, at all ages and in all weathers.

Young kittens need access to a litter tray as they should not be allowed out of doors until their inoculations are complete. Older kittens cannot always 'hold on' until they are allowed outside; elderly cats often become incontinent. Cats should always be kept indoors at night and so should be supplied with a tray. A cat's waste products are often the first indication that the cat is unwell, so the owner who supplies a litter tray will be able to take immediate action when a change is noticed. For all these reasons, a constantly available litter tray is vital.

There are three basic types of cat litter. The biggest-seller is made of dried clay. Next most popular are the wood-based litters and catching up fast is a litter made from pelletised corncobs!

The cat litter industry started in the United States in 1947 where it is now worth more than $300 million per year. It was developed by one man, Ed Lowe, who was selling industrial absorbents when a neighbour asked him for some sand for her cat's litter tray. Ed Lowe suggested dry clay instead and soon the neighbour would use nothing else. This gave Lowe the idea of bagging the clay and selling it. Unsure that anyone would pay for clay while sand was free, he suggested his local pet store should give it away. The rest, as they say, is history.

Glorious mud
First, the clay litters. These are the grey or white litters which you probably thought were manufactured, not realising their mineral origin.

Fullers' earth is the most popular, accounting for over half of all cat litter sales. In the United Kingdom, most of this is mined in Surrey, and is used throughout this country as well as being exported abroad. Fullers' earth has been used for centuries, long before cat litter was thought of. In Ancient Egypt, fashionable women used it as a hair cleanser (it is still a wonderful dry shampoo for cats!) and, hundreds of years ago, it was used in the northern woollen industry to remove grease from sheep's fleece. Mrs Beeton, in *Household Management*, suggested it should be used for cleaning carpets, scorched linen, a dusting powder for babies' bottoms and as a face-pack! Nowadays it is used as an ingredient in cosmetics and to absorb spilled oil in garages.

It is also the Paraquat antidote. The deadly poison, Paraquat, is absorbed by the Fullers' earth if the sufferer swallows it. Hopefully, the cat hasn't used it first.

The Surrey plant produces more than 170,000 tonnes of

clay each year, approximately one-third of which is destined for litter trays.

It is found in seams which can be as narrow as one metre in some places, buried beneath twenty metres of rock and sand. The quarrying machinery works along the seam, so the quarry is constantly moving – it is called a rolling hole. The deeper the Fullers' earth is found the better it is as cat litter. Clay found near the surface tends to be too soft. It is processed at a plant next to the quarry, where it is broken up, dried in temperatures from 200 °F to 1200 °F, and sieved to grade for size. The larger particles are used for cat litter, while smaller granules are used for other absorbent products. Within two or three hours of being dug from the ground, the clean, dry and still-warm litter can be on its way to the shops. As the quarry seam is used up, the land is restored to its original contours and replanted with grass and trees.

Fullers' earth has the technical name of *calcium montomorillonite*, although the technical names of litters often do not appear on the bag. One manufacturer of another type of clay, when asked why they did not state content on litter bags said: 'Most litters are natural minerals with rather complicated technical names which I am not sure many consumers would understand.'

Calcium montomorillonite, Fullers' earth (also known as 'grey' because of its colour) is made up of platelets giving a high internal surface area, which makes it extremely absorbent – it holds moisture up to 125 per cent of its own weight. Its advantages are that it is a cheap litter, it is excellent at absorbing smells (of both liquid and solid waste) and it forms a suspension in water. This means that small quantities can be flushed down the toilet, although disposal is seen as a problem with this type of litter. Disadvantages are the product's bulkiness and weight.

Moeler clay is another clay litter. It is pinkish-brown in colour and comes from Denmark. However, it is not widely used in the United Kingdom, being sold in only one group of supermarkets.

All clay litters go through a number of processes to help reduce dust, the bane of owners who hate having powdery pawprints throughout the house! Most manufacturers have been very successful in reducing clay dust to a large extent.

Cat litter and cancer

Can some types of cat litter cause lung cancer? This is a question which is currently concerning many owners.

Attapulgite is sometimes known as superwhite because of its pure white colour. Its atoms are arranged in clumps and it is imported from South Africa. It is lighter than calcium montomorillonite but not as absorbent.

Sepiolite is also white in colour, with a structure of atoms linked in long chains, enabling it to absorb moisture up to 110 per cent of its own weight.

Both *attapulgite* and *sepiolite* were linked in the August 1987 German Consumers' Council magazine, *Test*, with a risk of carcinogenity.

Test reported:

> The controversy centres on two frequently occurring components – attapulgite and sepiolite. The risk of carcinogenity arises when such products contain fibres with certain characteristics similiar to asbestos fibres which are now known to be definitely carcinogenic.
>
> To investigate the products, we asked our scientists to examine them under the electron scan microscope where their true nature becomes clear under a 10 to 29,000 fold magnification. They detected both granular and needle-shaped, fibrous material. *Only the*

needle-type fibres are suspected of causing cancer and only if they are at least one five-thousandth of a millimetre long.

In spite of the results obtained from the investigations, the German Consumer Council does not specifically label certain brands of cat litter as carcinogenic because one important criterion has not been investigated: *according to some experts, the solubility of the material also plays an important part and thin and pointed fibres would not be able to lodge in the lungs but would dissolve in the liquid present in the lungs and thus be rendered harmless.* Extensive tests on animals would be necessary to investigate this aspect and the German Consumer Council has neither the time nor the money; nor does it approve of such tests. [My italics.]

In other words, the white clay cat litters might be a factor in cancer in cats or they might not – but other types of litters such as calcium montomorillonite and the wood-based litters 'were found completely satisfactory' by *Test*. I would personally rather use a litter which was found 'completely satisfactory' than one which had any doubt hanging over it, although it has been stated by Dr J. C. Wagner, MD, FRCPath, on behalf of the Pneumoconiosis Unit of the Medical Research Council on 29 July 1987, that there is no medical evidence that cat litters containing sepiolite are harmful, either to humans or animals.

Litter deodorants

Some of the clay litters now have deodorants added to them which become effective as soon as the litter is used. These litters are obviously for the benefit of the owners; many cats don't like them at all and often problems of soiling outside the tray can be traced back to a change to this type of litter. Some cats even have an allergic reaction to them.

There are also deodorants available which are added to cat litter by the owner. Some rely on a fragrance to cover up odour while others change the shape of the odour molecule which triggers a response in the brain causing odour recognition – the smell is still there but your brain doesn't recognise it!

If you are concerned about odour, there are a number of things you can do without using deodorants or deodorised litter.

Place the litter tray in an out-of-the-way place (your cat will prefer it anyway), clean it out each time it is used (your cat will appreciate that too), provide a covered tray (see 'Litter trays', p. 83) and choose your litter for its natural deodorising properties.

Wood litters
If you remember sawdust on butchers' or pub floors, placed there to absorb spills, you might understand the popularity of wooden litters.

A growing percentage of the cat litter market is being taken over by wood-based litters. These are softwoods which have been turned into sawdust, dried, pelletised and bagged. They are incredibly absorbent, absorbing up to 300 per cent their own volume. Consequently, much less is used in the litter tray. Although clay litters are at their most efficient when used to a depth of 5–8 centimetres, wood litters should be spread over the tray in a very thin layer; they absorb so much liquid that they expand to several times their original size when wet.

Liquid releases their natural pine smells and these litters are particularly effective for liquid waste. The pellets turn back to sawdust when liquid is added to them. This 'sawdust' then dries out and cats often use it again. However, wood-based litters are not so effective when coping with solid waste; their odour-absorbing properties leave much to be desired. One great advantage with the wood-based litters is that they are completely biodegradable and can be tipped on to the compost heap or flushed down the toilet.

There is little dust with the wood-based litters and there have been reports of the condition of asthmatic cats improving when their litter has been switched to the wood-based type.

One other cat litter which is gaining converts in the United States and the United Kingdom is made from pelletised corncobs covered with a food-grade paraffin wax. Its little yellow granules are completely washable and reusable.

The granules come in a specially-designed tray with slots in the bottom of it and another tray underneath. If a cat urinates in the litter, the urine passes around the granules without being absorbed, and into the tray where it collects for emptying every few days.

The unit is initially expensive but virtually lasts for ever and is very effective. Its main disadvantage is that, although there is no smell from liquid waste which passes through the tray to the tray beneath (where all the smell is trapped), there are no deodorising properties for solid waste.

Since it is washable and non-absorbent, there is no litter medium to dispose of so this unit is ideal for apartment dwellers.

It is also useful if your vet asks you to collect a urine sample from your cat as the urine flows into the bottom tray, ready for collection. It beats standing waiting, jar in hand for the opportune moment.

Changing to a new litter
Cats are creatures of habit and some will resist when you change the type of litter in their tray. Others

will immediately leap on the tray to christen the new product.

If your cat resists, place some of the (clean) old type of litter on top of the new for a few days until it gets used to it. If your cat continues to resist, there may be a good reason why. Perhaps the new product is dustier and your cat does not like it, or perhaps there is something added to which your cat is allergic.

If you have persisted for several weeks and your cat simply will not use the new litter, you will have to give up and go back to the old.

Thousands of cats are provided with non-proprietary litter mediums such as torn-up newspaper, earth or cinders. These cost nothing, so are of benefit to anyone on a tight budget although the last two do have the disadvantage of dirtying paws and 'tracking' through the home.

Clay cat litters could be as much as 125,000,000 years old by the time they reach your cat's tray and they probably have a similar lifespan ahead of them. Which could mean displaying on the packets the warning: 'Sell by the year 125,001,990!'

Litter trays

Did you realise that cats like privacy just as much as we do when they go to the bathroom?

If your cat has been making do with an old seed tray for the last few years, you'll be amazed at the variety of litter trays now available, including those which allow it the privacy it needs.

Several manufacturers produce trays with tall covers, enabling the cat to climb inside through a small doorway. Cats like using these trays and owners like them too – they cut down on the litter scattered around the floor. The

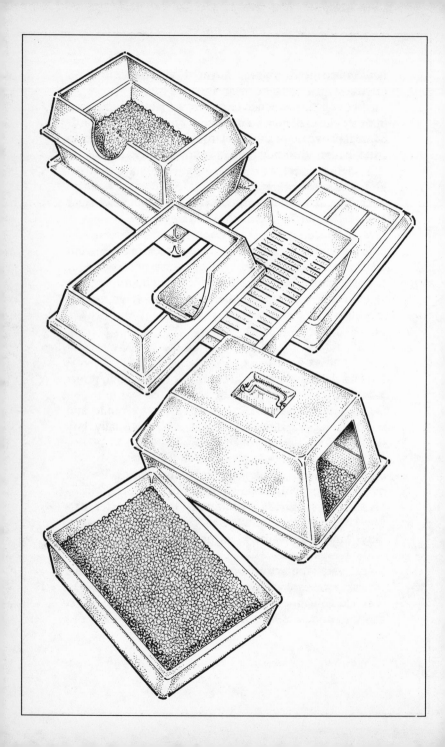

newest version combines a covered litter tray with a cat carrier – which must be confusing for a cat.

Although not expensive, you could devise a covered litter tray using an ordinary base with an upended cardboard box over it, or simply place the tray in a large box to cut down on scattering.

A slightly more sophisticated version has a charcoal filter inside, which absorbs odours for up to six months. According to the makers this means that sand, newspaper or gravel can be used as a litter medium.

Many owners still use the basic, inexpensive type of tray base and most cats have no objections to using them, but appreciate it if they are sited in a quiet, private spot. Some cats will happily use a tray sited in a cupboard and this suits their owners too, as there is less visible odour and mess.

Feeding bowls

Longhaired cats need larger feeding bowls than short-haired cats.

Pet shops sell a wide range of plastic, ceramic and stainless steel feeding bowls and owners usually buy whatever appeals to them aesthetically.

Several points should be taken into consideration. Remember to choose a bowl which is large enough – which means buying a larger bowl for a longhaired cat. This is because most cats will not eat from a bowl narrower than their whiskers (and longhaired cats have longer whiskers). They will trail their food on to the floor or pick it up with their paws rather than bend their whiskers.

Cats, like teenagers, can have spotty chins. Some cats have an allergic reaction to plastic bowls and this can make their chins spotty. In these cases, ceramic or stainless steel bowls should be chosen. In fact, ceramic or stainless steel bowls are much more hygienic than plastic and can be easily washed and sterilised.

It is also possible to buy disposable feeding bowls made specifically for pets, but ordinary paper plates will do just as well if you hate washing up.

High-tech has reached the world of cat bowls too. The latest models are automatic or semi-automatic feeders. Several work on a 'step up' principle; when a cat steps on a platform in front of the bowl a plastic lid tips up revealing food or drink. Food and water hoppers are available too, similar to those used for liquids in the cages of small mammals; dry cat food or water is gravity-fed into a bowl beneath.

For owners with irregular hours and cats with regular tummies there is an automatic feeder incorporating a refrigerator pack and a timer, which allows an owner to pre-set mealtimes for a housebound cat.

Other items make cat feeding easier too. Specially shaped pet food scoops get right down to the bottom of the tin and remove every bit of food. And if you don't use a full tin at a time, the remainder can be kept fresh by covering it with a pet food cap, which will also stop the odour permeating the refrigerator.

Scratching posts

Cats need to strop their claws on your furniture to prove that they live with you.

They're not being naughty when they shred the settee or claw the carpet – they're simply doing what comes naturally.

There are three reasons why a cat strops. First, it is part of a cat's territorial marking system. Scent glands on the paws mark whatever is being stropped with the cat's own scent and that tells other cats that this is his place.

Second, it performs a manicure. It shreds off the old part of the claw, keeping a cat's weapons in good shape.

Third, it is a form of kitty aerobics. Stropping is carried out in conjunction with stretching of the body, which helps the cat keep in trim.

Even cats which have access to a garden and natural scratching posts – trees – should have indoor posts for evening use or for use on those days when it is too wet to go outside.

Cats which are not familiar with scratching posts may not use one immediately. In that case, a demonstration by you usually gets the 'stropping instinct' going very quickly. Alternatively, gently rub the cat's paws over the post to give it the idea, backing this up by reprimanding it when it scratches the furniture.

A little catnip (see p. 93), rubbed on the post, will make it even more attractive to your cat than the new settee, and many commercially-made posts are now impregnated with catnip.

Posts come in many sizes and are covered in a variety of materials: carpet, rope, or low-priced 'disposable' posts of bark or cardboard. Some of the more expensive posts incorporate a perch on top for the cat to sit on and short arms with playballs – both features enjoyed by cats.

To enable a cat to stretch, a scratching post should be at least 75 centimetres high. Some posts fulfil this requirement many times over, by incorporating a ceiling-height climber with a scratching post. Shelves are provided at intervals and all cats enjoy climbing, stropping and chasing one another up and down these posts.

If you do not want the expense of a manufactured post, it is simple to make one yourself. A carpet offcut can be glued around any post with a sturdy base, or rope wound around it. Using carpeting means that you can match your room's colour scheme, but carpet does tend to shred and, if it is nylon-backed, the nylon fibres shred and can be swallowed by a cat.

For the mog with style, there is a range of designer scratching posts shaped like hedgehogs and tortoises with carved wooden faces and feet. And for kittens only, there is a mouse-shaped post so that junior can learn early which creature he is supposed to take out his aggressive tendencies on.

Cat flaps

One of the most common complaints about cats is that they won't use their cat flaps. Well, would you use a door if you had to bash it open with your head?

Flaps take varying degrees of effort to open; from 3 ounces to 18 ounces. If buying one, test the amount of pressure you need to exert to open it using one finger. Then pull your finger back at threshold level and see if it gets stuck in the flap. If it does, so might your cat's paw. Many cats have had their paw stuck in a cat flap which is another reason why they won't use them. A cat is less likely to trap a paw in a side-hinged flap than a top-hinged flap.

A third reason is that they cannot see what is outside before committing themselves to go through the flap. This is vitally important to any cat's sense of security and some manufacturers are responding to this by making flaps with clear plastic doors.

Another complaint is that strange cats use the flap to come indoors, steal food and cause damage. This problem can be avoided by installing an electronic or electro-magnetic cat flap. The cat then has a 'key to the door' worn on a collar around its neck. The electronic key transmits a signal which allows the door to open but, if your cat has a fast friend, it could pop indoors behind your cat and perhaps be unable to leave again until you return and let it out.

The electro-magnetic system has a key which activates a solenoid, unlocking the door. The flap is not selective, so will open to any cat wearing a magnetic collar. There have also been instances where pieces of wire, nails, and other metal debris have become tangled up in the collar, which could cause a cat harm.

Collars pose dangers in themselves, sometimes catching on branches and hanging or choking the cats wearing them. Cats often manage to wriggle out of them and a dedicated Houdini-cat would find itself unable to get indoors anyway.

Some simple cat flaps don't have a locking device; this is an optional extra. However, it is vital that a flap should lock so that you can keep track of your cat, keep it in at night, and keep other cats out.

To train a cat to use a cat flap, place the cat outside and prop the flap open. Call your cat and have a titbit handy to give your cat when it uses the flap. Leave the flap propped open until your cat becomes used to it, then close it just before feeding time when your cat is outside and call it in for its meal.

I prefer not to use a cat-flap at all as I like to know whether my cats are indoors or out, so it isn't a necessity by any means.

When installing a flap, follow the manufacturers' instructions and install at least 15 centimetres off the ground to allow easy access. If your door is unsuitable for installation (for example, toughened glass) flaps can be installed in some windows or even direct in the brickwork of a wall, with the aid of a builder.

Make sure that your cat flap is installed at more than arm's length from the doorlock. It has been known for burglars to put their arm through a cat flap and unlock the house door!

You can make your own flap by cutting a square in a door and fitting a hinged flap which can be operated by your cat or a sliding flap which can be left open or closed as necessary.

Sir Isaac Newton took advantage of DIY when his cat kept demanding to be let in or out while he was trying to work on his Fourth Law of Motion, or something equally important. Resourceful Sir Isaac cut a piece out of the bottom of the door. The cat later had kittens and Sir Isaac, it is rumoured, took care of the kittens' needs by cutting a smaller hole beside the first one!

Indoor or Outdoor Cat?

Should cats be kept indoors?

The typical picture of the moggy is of an animal which is as free as the wind; free to explore its outdoor territory and go about its mysterious business unhindered.

But freedom always entails a degree of risk and more and more cat-owners are finding that unacceptable. A survey commissioned in 1987 by an animal drugs company disclosed that half of all cats are killed in road accidents. Tens of thousands also go missing each year in the United Kingdom alone; many of which may have been stolen.

Cats can live perfectly happily with an indoor lifestyle, but this makes them totally dependent on their owners who must provide them with everything they need to lead a full and balanced life.

The life span of the average indoor cat is about twice that of the cat which goes outdoors, according to Dr Mike McMenomy of the Minneapolis Kitty Klinic. Another United States vet, Dr Louis L. Vine, agrees. He says that the lifespan of the completely outdoor cat averages only 6 years, while outdoor/indoor cats average 8 to 10 years. The completely indoor cat's average life span is 15 years.

Cat owners who live in high-rise apartments may have no other choice but to keep their cats indoors; owners who live in an area of busy road traffic or other hazards may feel their cats are safer indoors; and, in some cases, a cat itself might choose an indoor lifestyle. So how can an indoor cat be kept healthy and happy?

It will require a good diet, including some greenstuff; a

place in the sun; a comfortable sleeping-place; a private toilet area; somewhere to climb and hide; something to strop its claws on; companionship; and exercise and stimulation. All of these can be provided indoors by a caring owner.

An owner who lives in a small apartment will have to provide more for their cat's needs than one who lives in a large house. Stairs alone provide some exercise and a large home affords plenty of hiding, sleeping and play areas, as well as a change of scenery from room to room.

Check the 'Cat Kit' section (p. 72) for beds, bowls, litter and litter trays. It is more important for an indoor cat to be provided with equipment that it likes and will use than it is for an outdoor cat. For example, a cat which doesn't like the type of litter provided for it will, when it is allowed out of doors, use earth to cover up. An indoor cat doesn't have that option.

An indoor cat is also more in need of companionship than an outdoor cat which will choose its friends – and enemies! Some of that companionship can come from an owner but, unless the owner is at home almost all the time, the cat will become lonely at times. Acquiring a second cat for company for an indoor cat should be considered.

The condition of an indoor cat should be carefully monitored; if the cat's fur becomes dull or lifeless, the skin scaly, or the cat becomes nervous, listless or uninterested in its food or surroundings, it may need a vitamin supplement. A supplement specially formulated for cats can be obtained from vets or pet stores.

One thing an indoor cat misses is its access to growing plants. These are nibbled as an aid to digestion and to help get rid of unwanted matter, such as hairballs. Indoor cats are more likely to suffer from hairballs than outdoor cats, simply because of the lack of green matter. So why not grow your cat its own jungle? This is not only beneficial to the cat but can look attractive too.

Use a long, narrow planter, and fill this with pots containing sterilised potting compost. Grow grass in one pot as grass is the cat's favourite nibble when it has an upset stomach. Cocksfoot grass is the best type to grow for a cat and is usually available through pet stores or specialist cat equipment suppliers.

You can experiment with the contents of the other pots, growing wheat, oats or even budgie seed! One pot should contain catnip (also called catmint) which most cats find irresistible and which has a calming, relaxing effect upon them.

Catnip

Catnip has the same effect on cats whether they be moggies or lions and tigers. Five hundred catnip plants are being grown by a biologist in Devon in a last attempt to trap the 'Beast of Exmoor', a large black cat, believed to be an escaped puma, which is accused of killing sheep.

Catnip is a herb belonging to the mint family which was used in Ancient Egypt to soothe colic. Today, catnip tea is sold in health food stores as an aid to digestion. For a cat, it is a stimulant and relaxant combined.

Not every cat is susceptible to catnip; two or three cats out of every ten are not interested in it at all. The response is believed to be inherited. Kittens will not respond to it until the age of puberty, and will even try to avoid it up to the age of six to eight weeks. Susceptible cats behave like females in season; rubbing against the catnip, rolling, purring and generally having a good time!

The active chemical in catnip is nepetalactone which works upon the cat's nervous system. The response is activated by smell, although cats often eat it as well, and this does them no harm.

Although it can be purchased in dried form from herbalists, health food stores and pet stores, it can also be grown from seed. *Nepeta cataria* is the type you should grow, rather than the ornamental varieties, which do not contain nepetalactone and will have no effect on your cat.

It can be grown in pots (or outdoors from May and June) although it is not an easy plant to grow until the root system is established. It doesn't need a particularly rich soil, although a sunny position is favoured.

If transplanting, be careful not to crush the leaves, as this will release the scent which attracts cats and you may discover your seedlings disappear. You may have to protect the plants from cats until they are of a sufficient size to survive the occasional nibble. The plants attract bees but no destructive pests as their scent repels insects.

Harvest the plants, if your cat has not eaten them all, when they are about 45 centimetres tall, as this is when they contain the most concentrated amount of oil in the leaves. Catnip can be dried in the same way as any other herb, and should be stored in airtight jars (old coffee jars are ideal) away from direct light, until needed.

Catnip has many uses, as it will excite a cat, prompting it to play, but at the same time has a relaxing effect. It is not harmful to a cat and not addictive, but it does affect the cat's nervous system, so outdoor cats given catnip should be kept indoors until the effect wears off, which takes about half an hour.

It can be used in many ways: as an occasional treat, to persuade your cat to use a scratching post (rub catnip on the post), as a bribe to persuade your cat to climb into its basket for a trip to the vet's, and to perk up appetite by occasionally sprinkling a little on food. It makes a wonderful stuffing for cat toys. Owners should remove catnip toys from their cats after fifteen or twenty minutes' play and keep the toys in an airtight container. A cat's reaction to catnip diminishes if it is given too often and the catnip itself loses its essential oils and its smell over a period of time.

Strangely enough, this catnip response is duplicated (in some cats) by at least two fruits: the melon and the olive. Given either of these fruits, susceptible cats will behave as though they are in season, rolling, rubbing and showing pleasure. Apparently even wood from the olive tree has the same effect.

Valerian is another garden plant which attracts cats and produces an excited reaction in them. But do be careful what you grow in your garden. In Bournemouth, a seven-year-old cat was found staggering around. Police suspected that someone in the area was growing marijuana and the cat had eaten some!

Should cats be declawed?

Declawing is the surgical removal of a cat's claws, usually carried out to protect an owner's furniture. In the United Kingdom, veterinary associations make known their abhorrence of the practice and it is unlikely that a British vet would carry out the operation. In the United States, however, the procedure is not uncommon.

Declawing is not the same as having your fingernails trimmed; it is the equivalent, on a human, of having your fingernails removed down to the end of the first knuckle on each finger.

It is a disfiguring operation which leaves a cat feeling defenceless and unable to grip or climb. Some declawed cats suffer severe emotional trauma and can become deeply distrustful of their owners and their vets and may start biting. There is pain after the operation for the cat, risk of infection or haemorrhage and it is possible for the claw to regrow, necessitating a further operation.

It is also possible to have coloured beads fitted over a cat's claws to prevent it stropping. They must be uncomfortable for the cat – they are certainly unnatural – and caring owners will not use them. A properly trained cat will strop on the furniture very little, and most cat-lovers believe that slightly ragged furniture is a small price to pay for sharing their homes with cats.

Outdoor/indoor cats will strop out of doors as well as in the home but the indoor cat can only strop its claws indoors, so a good scratching post is vital for an indoor cat. If your cat has little opportunity for indoor climbing, one of the floor-to-ceiling climbing posts which doubles as a scratching post and incorporates shelves at different heights will become your cat's own 'tree'. It will not only help exercise its muscles, it will give it somewhere high and secure to perch and sleep.

You should trim your indoor cat's claws regularly (see 'Moggy Maintenance', p. 169). Stropping will hone any cat's claws to needle sharpness but, because indoor cats don't walk on hard surfaces like pavements and roads, there is nothing to wear them down again.

How can a cat be kept safe outdoors?

Your cat doesn't need total freedom to enjoy the great outdoors. It can enjoy the warmth of the sun, the delights of a breeze and the scents of outdoors from a secured windowsill.

It simply isn't safe to allow a cat to sunbathe unprotected on a high windowsill as so many have fallen to injury or death. But with a little woodworking skill, a windowsill protector can be made to allow your cat a taste of the outdoors. It's basically a box shape, the same width as a window, with a solid bottom and wire mesh on four sides. The remaining side is left open and the box is placed through a partly-opened window and secured on the inside. The cat gains access to it through the open side and can sunbathe on the sill in perfect safety, coming indoors again if the weather turns cold.

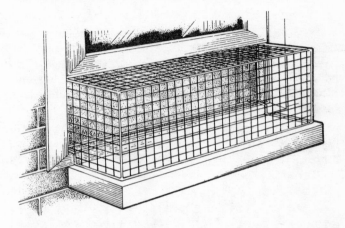

Balconies can be given a similar treatment. If completely enclosed with wire mesh they provide very safe, outdoor enclosures for cats.

If you have a garden, you can purchase a portable pen from cat equipment suppliers for your cat's sunbathing sessions. These are made of a sturdy wire mesh and are available up to 150 centimetres in length by 60 centimetres wide. If the base is left off, your cat can have access to grass for nibbling. They can be used in other ways too; as kittening pens or quarantine pens if a cat is ill.

There are also a number of specialist companies which will build an outdoor run in your garden. These are usually of wire mesh on timber construction and are often sunk into concrete bases. They have the advantage that they can be built to any size and can incorporate a cat chalet for your cat to shelter in. They could also be built around an existing tree in your garden, allowing your cat to climb and strop while in its run.

Some owners have completely fenced in their gardens for their cat's safety; adding an inward-facing mesh 'baffle' to the top of their fences which their cats cannot negotiate. Fences should be at least 185 centimetres tall and the baffle should face inwards at an angle of 45

degrees. The baffle must continue around any overhanging trees as a cat may try to climb a tree or garden shed in order to jump over the fence.

The least expensive option is to train your cat to wear a harness and leash. Attach a washing-line at both ends to low, secure objects then slip the leash over it, attach the leash to your cat's harness and it can roam up and down the garden along the length of the washing-line. This should, of course, only be done under supervision.

Better still, train your cat to take you for a walk!

How to take your cat walkies

Cats *can* be trained to walk on a leash although some will walk where you want and some will always walk where they want!

As with most things, it is easier to train a younger cat but, with patience, older cats will learn leash-training in time. It isn't true that moggies won't learn to walk on a leash; many enjoy this form of exercise.

Start with a collar. If your cat doesn't already wear one, you will have to get it used to having one on. Call your cat over, give it a treat to eat and, while it is munching, slip the collar round its neck. It should look quite tight but you must be able to slip one finger between collar and neck. If you can't, you're choking your cat. If you can slip several fingers between, the collar is too loose and your cat may trap its paw in it if it tries to push the collar off. Give your cat another treat or two, to take its mind off the collar.

Keep the collar on for around five or ten minutes, according to whether your cat accepts it or not, then take it off, giving your cat another treat. Repeat this the following day allowing the collar to remain on your cat for a longer period each time. When your cat is completely happy wearing the collar, it is time to get it used to a harness.

Cats cannot be taken for walks with a collar and leash as they are clever at slipping out of a collar. There are harnesses made specially for cats and these are in the shape of a letter H. One leg of the H goes around the cat's neck and is fastened with a buckle and the other 'leg' goes around the cat's back and buckles under the stomach. One cheaper type of harness has loops which you have to slip over your cat's head and legs. Because the fastener slides along the loops, it is less secure than the type which can be buckled, and cats are not keen on having their legs inserted through the second loop.

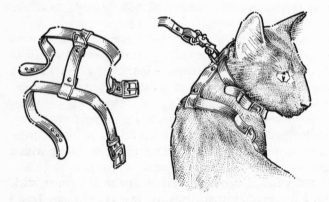

Remove your cat's collar and fasten the harness in position. Use treats to distract your cat while fastening it for the first few times. Again, leave the harness on for only a few minutes, building up the time day by day. When your cat is perfectly happy with the harness, you can try attaching the lead. Hold it loosely and stand as far away from your cat as you can, calling it to you. Reward it with a treat. After it has learnt to do this, you can then start walking slowly, calling the cat along with you and giving it a reward from time to time.

This is an ideal way to exercise your cat in a garden, although some cat owners have trained their cats to the leash so successfully that they can take them anywhere with them.

Playing with your cat

Although dog owners will play with their dogs throughout their pets' lives, many cat owners never consider playing with their pets.

Kittens are naturally active, with an almost insatiable desire for play but, as cats get older they may become lazier and play less and less. But play keeps cats healthier by toning their muscles and strengthening their cardio-vascular systems. It also helps them cope better with stress. A cat can become lethargic through inactivity. Play is particularly beneficial to an indoor cat. If an owner has a regular play session with their cat, the bond between pet and owner is strengthened.

Try to keep your play session to the same time each day, not immediately after a meal. Spend ten to twenty minutes playing with your cat, starting and finishing with a gentle warm-up and cool-down.

Roll a ball for your cat to chase, or twist a paper 'stick' for it to run after; many cats will learn to retrieve. Trail a dressing-gown cord for it to pounce on or use a fishing-rod type of toy; tie some stout, non-fraying string to a pole and tie a piece of tough fabric to the other end for your cat to chase while you sit in your chair holding the rod.

Cats love to chase moving objects and odd-shaped items roll erratically, making the chase more fun. Your cat may enjoy playing with any of the following: empty plastic 'lemons', egg-shaped plastic containers, walnuts, plastic drinking cups, empty toilet rolls, the washed caps from aerosol sprays, pine cones, wine corks and practice plastic golf balls.

Save empty sewing-cotton reels and string several together with a loop of cord. Securely thread a variety of buttons on a strong cord and hang it up for your cat to bat and catch. If you have any scraps of fur fabric, cut them into tubes 10–20 centimetres long and stuff them with catnip. Toys don't have to look like mice to be fun!

And, if you sometimes finish your own aerobics exercises with a massage, you can learn to massage your cat! This helps relieve stress for animals just as much as humans, and can even help relieve the effects of some ailments such as cystitis, arthritis and kidney problems.

Never use oil when massaging a cat and always stroke in the direction of the fur. Do not touch the backbone or windpipe when massaging.

Place your cat on your lap and slowly stroke it from head to tail until it begins to relax. Then, with the flat part of the fingertips, gently massage along its sides, using small, circular movements, from neck to tail. Then, using the same circular movements, massage the back of the neck and stroke the front of the neck with vertical movements (but not the windpipe). Then gently stroke the legs between your fingers in a downward movement and gently massage between each pawpad, jiggling each toe. Finish by using circular movements on the tummy and gently caressing all over.

If massaging a cat seems a fairly nutty pastime to you, consider that there are now Japanese health farms for pets, where cats are taught yoga. Apparently, their biggest challenge is to master breathing properly!

Feline Food

Convenience foods

It has never been easier to feed our cats a balanced diet. Canned cat food, introduced into the United Kingdom in the 1930s, revolutionised pet keeping, and now accounts for around 80 per cent of all pet food sold.

Supermarkets have taken over the roles of the 'cat-meat man' and the family butcher and fishmonger who would once have provided cheap scraps for pet food. Between 1970 and 1983, the price of butchers' meat increased by 362 per cent, yet in the same period prepared pet food increased in price by only 173 per cent. This makes canned food extremely good value for money.

It is now an important factor in the supermarkets' price wars and they devote as much as 9 per cent of their selling space to pet foods. And sales are helped along by an advertising expenditure for tinned food of more than £13 million per year in the United Kingdom.

Very few owners feed their cats on scraps nowadays. Butcher's or fishmonger's scraps are hard to come by and leftovers from human meals become scarcer as food becomes more expensive. Those who do prepare their cat's food themselves tend to be older owners who have more time available and who were brought up before tinned food (for humans and pets) became commonplace.

In 1984, a cat magazine surveyed its readers and asked what they wanted from cat food: 25 per cent said that cost was the most important criterion when choosing cat food; 54 per cent stated that nutritional value was the most important criterion and 7 per cent queried the use of additives in cat food.

Additives such as preservatives and colourings are included in cat food for *our* benefit – not for our cats' who don't actually care what the food looks like or how long it keeps fresh.

So what do cats like to eat?

Cats have very definite dietary preferences and will often choose for themselves foods which contain the nutrients which they require, if they have free access to it. They have a very high requirement for protein – possibly higher than any other creature – and they will choose high-protein content food over an equally palatable, but lower-protein content one. They will also enjoy fat, which will provide them with energy, either in the form of fat on meat, or cream. The B vitamins can be important to the cat's well-being and a cat will often choose food rich in thiamin. Well-fed cats can often be spotted scavenging in dustbins and eating the decaying contents. I don't believe they are being perverse in doing so. It's more likely that they are instinctively searching out sources of required nutrients, such as vitamin K, found in decaying meat, but otherwise lacking in many modern cat's diets.

How do cats 'select' their food? Movement is important for those cats which catch prey as food but otherwise the appearance of food is unimportant to cats. It is believed that a cat's perception of colour is not as acute as ours, so any colouring added will not make the food more attractive to a cat. Their eyesight is not good close-to, so smell is of more importance in attracting a cat to food than vision. Texture is relatively unimportant to cats as they will eat the hardest of dry food as readily as food with a very high moisture content.

What is most important to a cat is flavour, smell (which is more closely allied to the taste sense in the cat than in humans) and temperature.

Serving temperature is important for a cat's acceptance of almost any food – the nearer it is in temperature to that of freshly-killed prey, the more easily it will be accepted. Therefore refrigerated food should be allowed to warm up before serving. A few seconds in the microwave oven will make cold food more appealing.

The cat's senses of taste and smell are remarkably acute, enabling them to pick out any foreign body in their food (such as pills or tablets) without any difficulty. The Jacobson's organ allows a cat to taste and smell at the same time, so cats which are unable to smell their food due to a blocked nose or other illness, will become uninterested in food. Feeding strong-smelling food such as pilchards or sardines to an ill cat will help; as will mixing strong-smelling additives such as Marmite or a beef stock cube, with the cat's regular food.

Cats will enjoy a food which smells and tastes good to them and many owners will interpret this as being the 'best' food for them. This is far from true. Some cats, if allowed, would eat liver exclusively, resulting in a dangerous overdose of vitamin A. Liver content of a cat's diet should never exceed 10–20 per cent.

In the case of prepared foods, manufacturers spend large sums of money on research into palatability – ensuring that cats will enjoy the taste and smell of their foods. Additives are used to enhance flavour and smell. These, although indetectable to humans, send out potent signals to cats, who seem to prefer the foods containing their favoured additives, although these will not enrich the food nutritionally.

Cats will become firmly entrenched in habit. If fed one particular food exclusively, they may become resistant to change. It is most important, when changing a cat's diet, for any reason, that it be done gradually. To start with, the new food should be mixed into the cat's regular food in very small quantities. These quantities can be increased slowly until the cat is eating nothing but its new diet; this could take several months in the case of a particularly resistant cat. A cat will refuse a new food it dislikes for a very long time, so a rapid changeover can lead to virtual starvation by the cat. Even if a cat is willing to change its diet, this should be done slowly as diarrhoea will inevitably follow a rapid diet change. It is best to accustom a cat to a wide variety of foods from kittenhood; this often stops cats from developing into fussy feeders.

There are factors which govern the cat's feeding, other than the palatability, smell, temperature and habit. If you have difficulty with feeding your cat, some of the following points may have a bearing.

Remember that the cat must be able to smell its food and that the temperature of the food should be as near blood heat as possible. The place designated as your cat's eating area is important. It should be somewhere relatively quiet where the cat will not run the risk of being tripped over while eating. Many cats like to eat privately, without other people or cats around. 'Mother' cats should be fed separately from their weaned kittens – their instincts can lead them to deprive themselves of food in favour of their kittens – even when these kittens have become adults.

Cats should have their own feeding bowl, used for no other purpose, and in a household of more than one cat each cat should have its own bowl. Bowls should be wider than the cat's whiskers, otherwise the cat may trail the food on to the floor. (Another reason for this is if the food is in large lumps – the cat will cut it up with its teeth on the floor.) Cats will not enjoy using bowls which are dirty or which smell strongly of washing-up liquid (baking soda in the final rinse will eliminate smells). Disinfectant (other than a hypochlorite product such as diluted Domestos) should never be used as it can be toxic to cats.

Bowls should be kept in a different room to the litter tray. Some cats also prefer their water bowl to be in a different room to their feeding bowl. Most finicky eaters become less fussy if another cat is introduced into the household, or if their food bowl is removed, empty or not, ten to fifteen minutes after feeding.

Lack of appetite may be due to a nutritional deficiency or illness, so veterinary advice should be sought for a cat which stops eating for no apparent reason.

What's in the tin?

A lot of cat lovers love other animals too and are very concerned that their pets might be eating creatures which neigh, hop or perform in Judy Collins' songs. In the United Kingdom, this is very unlikely.

The Pet Food Manufacturers' Association represents manufacturers who account for 95 per cent of British pet food sales. The PFMA states quite clearly that none of its members use horse, pony, kangaroo or whale meat in the manufacture of pet food.

What animal-based protein the industry uses comes almost entirely from 'those parts of the carcase that where custom and usage dictate they are unsuitable for human consumption. That material, if not used in the manufacture of pet foods would otherwise be wasted and the rest of the carcase would be proportionately more expensive.' So there is no need to feel guilty about feeding meat to your pets – they are not depriving any human of a nutritionally sound diet.

The contents of a prepared cat food vary from day to day, due to the supply situation of the raw materials. They will contain meat and meat by-products – and if the food is labelled as 'flavoured' the meat in it will not necessarily be the meat mentioned – which are all the fleshy parts of animals and derivatives of the processing of the carcase. This will include products such as offal from abattoirs and poultry factories which has been deemed unfit or unsuitable for human consumption, including frozen and dried blood, fish trimmings and ground bone for calcium.

There may also be extruded vegetable protein, as animal protein becomes more expensive, which can come from the treatment of products such as cereals, vegetables, pulses and oil seeds.

Cereal may be included, especially in the cheaper foods, as well as vitamin concentrates to replace those lost in the manufacturing process, and possibly gelling agents, colouring and flavouring.

Contents are listed on the container and you should look for a food which is marked as 'complete'; a few prepared foods, for example, the chubs (sausage-shaped, plastic-wrapped, meat-based food), are not complete food. A cat fed entirely on an incomplete food would not enjoy top condition and may become ill.

Nutrition for cats

Makers of cat foods recommend the amount which should be fed on the can or packet. The average-size adult cat requires 350 kilocalories each day, which is three times as many calories, weight for weight, as its owner. Feed your cat two or three small meals per day, if possible, rather than one big meal. But don't overdo it like the woman in Wales who owned the United Kingdom's biggest cat – it weighed 14 kilogrammes and had a 78-centimetre waistline!

If you feed your cat a proprietary complete food, you

needn't worry about feline nutrition (the manufacturers and their nutritionists worry about it for you) and can turn to the next section.

But, if you would like to know more about the subject, or if you do not always feed your cat a proprietary complete food, the following section attempts to explain the subject to the best of present-day knowledge. However, the cat, being a complex creature with specialised dietary needs which we are still discovering, may still be hiding some secrets from us all.

Note: 1,000 mg (milligrams)   = 1 g (gramme)
            1,000 mcg (micrograms) = 1 mg (milligram)
            IU   International Unit

Protein

Protein is built up from about twenty sub-units, called amino acids. These link up in different ways to form different types of protein. While protein is being digested in the body, the amino acids are absorbed into the blood-stream and used to reform new proteins. Protein, in the form of enzymes, is needed to keep the entire body functioning normally and, in addition, the body itself is largely made of protein. The cat can synthesise about ten amino acids in its body but there are a further ten which the cat cannot make and these must be obtained directly from the diet. Therefore they are called 'essential' amino acids.

Meat and fish are excellent sources of all the amino acids, and cooking improves the digestibility of protein. Grains, although less-good quality protein sources, low in one or more amino acid, can be utilised by the cat.

Thus there are different 'qualities' of protein, graded according to essential amino acid content. Those with the most essential amino acids are eggs and milk, with meat and fish also rich protein sources. These are the top quality proteins. If the diet is adequate in all nutrients, carbohydrates and fats will supply energy, but protein is also used to supply energy and provides 4 calories (also called kilocalories or kcal) of usable energy per gram. If their diet is too low in protein, cats use their own body-protein to supply energy and consequently waste away, even if given plenty of carbohydrate or fat. The recommended dietary intake is at least 28 per cent of the dry matter of the diet, of which at least half should be of animal origin. This is nearly twice the maintenance protein need of a dog.

There is also a substance similar to an amino acid, called *taurine*, which is an essential component of a cat's diet. Although the dog can synthesise sufficient taurine from two amino acids, the cat cannot, so taurine must be obtained directly from the diet. It is found mainly in animal products and seafood. Commercial dog food may not contain sufficient for a cat's use, so cats regularly fed some dog foods (or cats on vegetarian diets) will develop a deficiency, which will lead to retinal lesions and irrevocable blindness.

Fat

Fat is important in the diet as a concentrated form of energy, providing 9 calories of usable (metaboliseable) energy – the amount absorbed by the cat's body – per gram. Fat also transports the fat soluble vitamins and other important substances around the body. Dietary fat is needed as a source of the essential fatty acids (EFAs).

These substances are converted in the body to prostaglandins which help to control vital body processes. Unlike other mammals, cats cannot utilise the EFAs, linoleic acid and linolenic acid. They require arachadonic acid and other polyunsaturates which occur only in animal fats or fish oils. These therefore must be supplied in the diet and only very small amounts are needed. Vegetable oils are useless to the cat as a source of EFAs but can, of course, supply calories.

A deficiency of fat can lead to eczema, damaged ovaries, sterility in the male, kidney damage and retarded growth.

Cats do not suffer from coronary artery disease, so addition of fat to the diet need not be feared. In fact, the addition of small amounts of fat to the diet will make it more attractive to the cat, similar to our spreading butter on bread, but it should not be used to replace protein.

In one case, a thirteen-year-old cat from Lancashire was showing the effects of her age and most of her fur fell out. Her vet recommended an increased fat intake. Every day, her owner coated her with melted margarine and the cat licked it off. After three months, the cat's fur grew back and she was the picture of health again.

Carbohydrate

Carbohydrate (starch and sugar) is not essential for the nutrition of the cat. It is contained in many commercial cat foods, mainly to 'bulk out' the food cheaply. It can be used as an energy source, providing 4 calories of usable energy per gram, but dietary fat can substitute more efficiently.

It is unlikely that cats in the wild would obtain a source of carbohydrate once weaned and the addition of carbohydrate to the diet may possibly slow down digestion and the passage of food through the gut.

Vitamins

Vitamins are organic substances which facilitate biological and chemical processes in the body.

They are present in both meat and plants but most of the

vitamins cats receive will be from animal sources and their diet should accommodate this.

There are dangers inherent in feeding too much of one particular food, for example liver (see 'Vitamin A') so variety is vitally important, not just to prevent boredom, but for health.

There are two sub-groups of vitamins: the fat-soluble vitamins such as A and D which are stored in the body. This means that a *daily* intake of these vitamins is not essential; the body will use what it requires from its stock. There is a particular risk of toxicity from fat-soluble vitamins if an overdose is given. The water-soluble B vitamins 'flush through' the body if an excess is taken, being excreted in the urine, but every attempt should be made to supply vitamins in the required proportions.

Vitamin A
Two important points about vitamin A should be borne in mind when feeding your cat.

1 Cats have a high requirement for vitamin A; estimated at between 1,000 and 2,000 IU (International Units) per day.

2 A cat can become very seriously ill if given too much vitamin A in its diet.

Retinol is the only useful form of vitamin A for a cat. Carotene is a precursor of vitamin A but is useless to cats as they are unable to convert it to vitamin A. Therefore, good sources of the vitamins for *humans* such as carrots, maize, broccoli and other leafy vegetables, provide no vitamin A for a cat.

Cats must obtain their vitamin A requirement from retinol, sometimes called vitamin A_1, from animal-derived sources. The vitamin is fat-soluble, not water-soluble, and does not wash through the body but is stored in the liver, which is why animal liver is such a good source of the vitamin. Fish liver is very rich in vitamin A and fish liver oil is an excellent source of the vitamin for a cat. Cheddar cheese, cream and egg yolk are also good sources.

An important function of vitamin A is vision. The vitamin attaches to a protein in the cells of the retina and the molecule is altered by light which stimulates nerves, transmitting an impulse to the brain which is then 'seen'.

Vitamin A is also needed for healthy skin and membranes, sound teeth, for bone growth in a young cat, and is important in reproduction.

Lack of the vitamin can result in blindness, conjunctivitis, ulceration of the cornea, blockage of the bronchial tubes, and a form of keratosis – a roughening of the skin.

An excess of the vitamin is dangerous – it can lead to distorted bones and lameness in a young cat along with massive deposits in the liver and kidney, plus stiffness, gingivitis and tooth problems in an older cat. This happens most often when a cat is fed a diet high in liver. The cat can become addicted to its unhealthy diet, making treatment difficult. Surgery may even be needed to remove bony outgrowths.

Commercially prepared cat food will usually have vitamin A added to it in the correct quantities, but the vitamin is sensitive to light and oxygen and is destroyed by rancid fats. Therefore, tinned foods should not be kept more than a day once opened and they should be covered and kept refrigerated to prevent deterioration. Pork, lamb, white fish and cereal or potatoes are poor sources of the vitamin, so some supplementation with a few drops of fish liver oil may be necessary if a cat's diet contains a high proportion of these foods.

Liver, if liked, can be fed once a week and two ounces will give a cat its weekly requirement of the vitamin. Cod liver oil contains about 3,000 IU of vitamin A per teaspoonful, so three teaspoonfuls will give a cat its weekly requirement.

A cat receiving a small amount of liver once a week, along with a well-balanced meat-derived diet, would not require fish liver oil or any other vitamin A supplement.

Vitamin D
Vitamin D is a fat-soluble vitamin which, if given to excess, can lead to bone being dissolved and absorbed and even death. It is necessary for absorption of calcium and the strengthening of bones with calcium and phosphorus.

Fatty fish such as sardines, herring and mackerel are an excellent source of the vitamin, as is fish liver oil. Commercially-prepared cat food will usually have vitamin D present in the correct proportions; a cat's requirement is around 100 IU per day.

A cat which is allowed out of doors may synthesise the vitamin on its skin. Irradiation from sunlight will form vitamin D from oils on the coat or skin which will then be licked off by grooming. An indoor cat will not form vitamin D from sunlight, even if sitting by a sunny window, as ultra-violet light cannot come through the glass. It is a good idea to provide an 'indoor' cat with a safe wire mesh run in the garden which he can use on sunny days. For flat-dwellers, a wire mesh screen can be made to fit a window opening. The cat will remain safely indoors but will receive the benefits of sunshine.

Although a deficiency in this vitamin can cause rickets in a kitten, it is rare, as it appears that kittens can store and use vitamin D which they have received from their mother's milk.

It is more important that the ratio of calcium and phosphorus in the diet is correct, for, if extra vitamin D is given to a cat which is deficient in calcium, it will promote bone resorption, making the condition worse.

A cat receiving a balanced diet and able to lie in the sun would not require a supplement, but could be fed one meal of an oily fish occasionally.

Vitamin E

The most vital function of vitamin E is in curbing the oxidation and consequent rancidity of unsaturated fatty acids. It is held in cell membranes and is required for normal membrane function. Red blood cells may be slightly less robust if the vitamin is deficient. It has been found essential for healthy reproduction in cats and many people believe it has beneficial effects beyond what can actually be proved for it!

The daily requirement depends on the level of unsaturated fatty acids; the more of these which are absorbed, the higher the requirement for vitamin E. Cats fed on diets containing little vitamin E can develop steatitis, also called yellow fat disease, which may follow the feeding of too much oily fish. There is a range of other disorders which may follow from a deficiency of vitamin E and which affect the muscular, reproductive, vascular and nervous systems.

A cat's daily requirement for vitamin E is uncertain, but is approximately 8 IU per day – more if a high level of unsaturated fat is fed. Eggs, vegetable oils and wheatgerm oil capsules made specifically for cats are available. The vitamin can help accelerate the healing of wounds, so would probably be found useful by the owners of scrapping tomcats!

Cats should not be given too much of the vitamin as in many animals it leads to possible sterility and slower clotting of blood.

Vitamin K

This is known as the coagulating vitamin and deficiency impairs the body's blood-clotting mechanism.

A cat's supply of the vitamin is synthesised by beneficial bacteria inhabiting the digestive system. The vitamin is not stored in the body to any great extent and a deficiency can arise, if, for example, antibiotics are given which will destroy the gut bacteria. Although the vitamin is found in many green leafy vegetables, the best sources for a cat are probably liver, fish liver oils – and decaying prey! Eating decaying meat is not such a health hazard as might be at first supposed as animal protein passes rapidly through the cat's gut, in approximately twenty-four hours, although, of course, it is not recommended that you deliberately feed your cat obviously decayed meat. So if you see your cat chasing more than his fair share of mice or birds after a course of drug treatment, he is actually doing something essential to his health.

Large quantities of vitamin K may cause anaemia but it is difficult to provide an overdose of this vitamin.

Vitamin B complex
B complex vitamins are water soluble and, as such, it is unlikely that an overdose could be given. If taken in quantities larger than the body needs, the excess is 'flushed through' the system and excreted in the urine. The B vitamins often occur in the same types of foods, and more importantly, occur in the correct ratio. They also complement each other's action so a good diet is most important. Liver is a rich source of the B vitamins but care should be taken not to feed your cat too much liver as it may lead to an overdose of vitamin A. Yeast is also a good source and Brewers Yeast tablets can be given to your cat as a daily treat, or yeast spread (Marmite) can be added to food.

These vitamins are necessary for the utilisation of foods and to provide energy and control protein synthesis with B_{12} also being needed for nerve function.

Thiamin

Also called vitamin B_1, 0.5 mg (milligrams) is the recommended daily dietary intake of thiamin for the cat. A deficiency can lead to anorexia, heart failure and even death. Pork, bacon, heart and kidney are all good sources and 200 g or less will supply the dietary requirement. Less thiamin is required if a cat is fed a diet high in fat and low in carbohydrate than if the cat is fed a high carbohydrate diet. Therefore, if you bulk out your cat's food with potato, rice, pasta or bread, an additional source of thiamin must be given to make good any deficiency, for example by giving yeast tablets. Fish, if fed, should always be lightly cooked. Raw fish contains an enzyme, thiaminase, which inactivates thiamin, and can reduce the availability of thiamin from other foods by as much as half. Sulphur dioxide, used sometimes as a preservative, also destroys thiamin. Cats will show a preference for foods rich in thiamin if given a choice.

As cooking also destroys thiamin, commercially prepared foods are supplemented with a large quantity, so that sufficient remains after processing to meet recommended dietary levels.

Riboflavin

Also called vitamin B_2, 0.5 mg is the recommended daily dietary intake of riboflavin for the cat. Liver, kidney, cheese and eggs are all good sources. Milk is also a good source of riboflavin but it is interesting to note that half the vitamin is lost in just a few hours if milk is left sitting on the doorstep in sunlight in a glass bottle, as riboflavin is destroyed by ultra-violet light. A very tiny amount of liver or kidney will supply the dietary requirement of riboflavin, as will 300 g of milk. Deficiency can lead to skin and eye problems, anorexia and consequent loss of weight.

Pantothenic acid

Once called vitamin B_3, 1 mg is the recommended daily dietary intake. As pantothenic acid is found in all foods, a deficiency is unlikely in a well-balanced diet. A deficiency can lead to lack of growth and intestinal problems. Yeast and liver are good sources of the vitamin and little more than 10 g of liver will supply the dietary requirement. About a third of pantothenic acid is lost when meat is cooked and a third or more can be lost when meat is tinned.

Nicotinic acid

Also called niacin, 4.5 mg a day is the recommended dietary intake. The cat is unusual in that it cannot convert efficiently the amino acid, tryptophan which is available in most proteins, to nicotinic acid, and so has an absolute requirement. As liver, meats, fish, cheese and eggs are good sources, a deficiency is not likely. 20 g of liver or 70 g of fish will supply the dietary requirement. A deficiency leads to ulcers and inflammation of the mouth. Nicotinic acid is a stable vitamin and little or none is lost during cooking.

Pyridoxine

Also called vitamin B_6, 0.4 mg a day is the recommended dietary intake. A deficiency can lead to a type of anaemia and kidney damage. Most foods contain small amounts of pyridoxine and yeast, liver, kidney and other meats and fish are good sources. It is very unlikely that a cat fed on a balanced diet would suffer a deficiency, but if a deficiency exists, it is exacerbated by a high protein diet, in the same way a deficiency of thiamin is exacerbated by a high carbohydrate diet. About one third of the vitamin is lost when meat is cooked, so feeding raw meat occasionally could be a useful source.

Biotin
5 mcg (micrograms) is the recommended dietary intake. Biotin is found in most foods, and is synthesised in the intestine. A deficiency will lead to dermatitis, and is possible after a course of antibiotics (which will kill beneficial gut flora as well as harmful bacteria) or if *raw* egg white is fed. Raw egg *yolk*, raw white contains avidin which combines with biotin making it unavailable for absorption into the bloodstream. If your cat enjoys egg, it must be cooked.

Folic acid
100 mcg is the recommended daily intake. Folic acid is found in most foods and liver, yeast extracts and milk are the best sources. It is also synthesised in the intestine, so a deficiency is possible after a course of antibiotics. A deficiency can lead to anaemia. Folic acid is easily destroyed by processing or cooking meats, or boiling milk, so occasional raw meat can form a valuable addition to the diet.

Vitamin B$_{12}$
2 mcg is the recommended daily intake. The vitamin is widely available in many foods enjoyed by cats but if not adequately absorbed due to a lack of a substance made in the lining of the stomach (called intrinsic factor), a deficiency can arise leading to pernicious anaemia and degeneration of the insulating sheath of nerves. Liver, kidney, oily fish meats and eggs are good sources of the vitamin.

Choline
This has many important functions including the formation of phospholipids (components of cell membranes). 200 mg is the recommended daily intake, although adequate supply of methionine (an essential amino acid) can replace the need for choline. Choline nevertheless is in

generous supply in meat and eggs, less than half an egg supplying the dietary level. A deficiency can cause fat to accumulate in the liver.

Vitamin C

Also known as ascorbic acid, vitamin C can be synthesised from glucose in the diet by the cat in its liver. Unlike humans, the cat does not need a dietary source of this vitamin but it has been prescribed in some cases of Feline Urological Syndrome (see 'Magnesium') to acidify the urine.

Minerals and trace elements

You will find an odd word on the label of commercially prepared cat foods – 'ash'. This is actually the mineral content of the food.

'Ash' is what remains when the food is burned and consists, in the form of oxides or salts of the macrominerals – calcium, phosphorus, magnesium, sodium and potassium – and the microminerals (or trace elements) required in much smaller amounts and consisting of iron, iodine, copper, zinc, manganese etc.

These are essential to normal healthy growth in the correct quantities (see under individual headings for dietary needs). However, a high ash-content diet or a diet where the ratios are incorrect can cause problems and has been implicated in the occurrence of Feline Urological Syndrome.

Cats fed balanced home-prepared meals should receive the minerals they require from the food, as the food animal has eaten greenstuff containing these nutrients. This does not apply to calcium and a carefully chosen supplement will correct this deficiency.

Cats fed commercially prepared foods should have their

brand of food chosen with care, with particular reference to the ash content, which should be as low as possible, except for nursing queens, who have a higher mineral requirement.

Mineral supplements should be given only under veterinary advice as over-dosage can be extremely dangerous to your cat's health, and with some minerals a very tiny amount constitutes an over-dosage.

Calcium and Phosphorus

These minerals are stored in bone and cats living naturally would obtain their requirement by eating the bones of their prey. Calcium helps form strong, healthy bones, teeth and also aids blood clotting and nerve impulse transmissions. Phosphorus stabilises cell membranes and helps with the transfer of energy inside cells. Milk, cheese and yoghurt are good sources.

It is important that these minerals are in the correct ratio for cats, and are available in conjunction with sufficient vitamin D, which is necessary for their absorption. Recommended dietary intake is calcium 0.8 g, phosphorus 0.6 g per 100 g of dry diet.

Magnesium

Normally, some magnesium is absorbed into the bloodstream with some being excreted by the urine. The remainder is needed for normal nerve cell function and for utilisation of calcium and potassium.

A magnesium deficiency leads to depression, lethargy, weakness or even fits, but is rare. An excess of magnesium has been associated with Feline Urological Syndrome, an obstruction of the urinary tract by the formation of crystals of ammonium magnesium phosphate hexahydrate. The feeding of some 'dry' cat foods has been implicated in the formation of these crystals as the ash content tends to be high and the water content (which would help 'flush out' the system) is low. The recommended dietary intake of magnesium is about 40 mg a day. Wheatgerm is a good source.

Sodium

Sodium, in the form of common salt (sodium chloride), is required to maintain a constant body water content and along with potassium salts, is an electrolyte. Sodium is found in the extracellular fluids, blood and tears. Surplus sodium chloride is excreted in urine. Salt need not be added to a cat's food except under veterinary advice. Cats suffering from FUS (see above) are sometimes given a diet higher in salt to alleviate the symptoms by increasing water intake and urinary volume. Recommended dietary intake of sodium chloride is about 125 mg a day though higher levels are commonly fed without apparent harm to healthy cats.

Potassium

Potassium is necessary for the proper functioning of the body cells. Potassium deficiencies are rare but can occur after prolonged diarrhoea. Symptoms are weakness and apathy and lesions of some organs can occur. Dried milk and fish are good sources of potassium and the recommended dietary intake is about 0.4 g a day.

Iron

Iron is needed for red blood cell formation and is a component of haemoglobin which carries oxygen from the lungs to the tissues. Respiratory enzymes (cytochromes) contain iron and myoglobin, found in red muscles which also carry oxygen. Lack of iron leads to anaemia with its attendant tiredness and weakness. The body absorbs iron only when required; when not needed, most passes unabsorbed through the body and is excreted. As with other minerals, an overdose is toxic.

Red meat, liver and fatty fish are good sources of iron. Although soya beans are good sources of iron too, iron from foods of vegetable origin is less well absorbed than that from food of animal origin. Constituents such as phytic acid in vegetable foods render most of the iron unavailable for absorption and commercially prepared foods containing meat *and* vegetable derivatives (such as soya beans) may need to have a higher percentage of iron in them for the cat to receive its recommended dietary intake of about 10 mg.

Zinc
Zinc is required for healthy growth, good skin and wound healing. It also helps animals taste and savour their food. A recent study among human anorexics has correlated anorexia with a zinc deficiency. Certainly, cats with this deficiency can lose interest in food and become thin. Good sources are beef, lamb, liver, cheese and dried milk, and the best sources are wheatgerm and oysters! So Dr Johnson wasn't just being eccentric when he fed oysters to his cat, Hodge. The recommended dietary intake of zinc is about 3 mg a day.

Manganese
The importance of manganese is not fully understood but it is believed necessary for healthy bone growth, reproduction and a strong nervous system. Meat, fish, eggs and fat all contain small amounts of manganese, but milk is believed to contain none. Recommended dietary intake is about 0.5 mg a day.

Copper
Copper is necessary to release stores of iron from the liver and a deficiency can cause anaemia, even when iron

stores are high. It is also needed for the formation of healthy bone, skin and blood vessels, and for the formation of melanin, which colours skin and hair. Liver and shellfish are excellent sources of copper, and beef and yeast extract are good sources. Recommended dietary level is about 0.5 mg a day.

Iodine

The main function of iodine is as a component of substances manufactured by the thyroid gland which controls the body's metabolic rate. It is important during growth, and pregnancy. Sea fish is one of the few sources of iodine but much of this can be lost during cooking in water. Cook fish in as little water as possible and pour the fishy water over the fish or over cereal as a morning meal. Recommended dietary intake is about 35 mcg a day.

Others

A tiny amount of selenium is required in a cat's diet as it has been discovered that it can prevent some of the symptoms of vitamin E deficiency, with which it has a close inter-relationship, although it has a separate function. It is thought it can protect the body against some poisons and may even be an anti-carcinogen. British meat will contain adequate selenium supplies as the animal will have absorbed selenium from its fodder as the occurrence of selenium is sufficiently high. Again, over-dosage is extremely dangerous and this mineral first came to attention because of its toxicity in high-selenium areas of the United States. Recommended dietary intake is about 10 mcg a day.

Also needed in very small amounts, cobalt is utilised as part of the vitamin B_{12}. No additional cobalt may be required as long as there is an adequate supply of the vitamin.

A few other trace elements in very small amounts may be necessary for the health of cats, although this has not been established.

A good, *varied* diet including prey meat, if possible, should provide trace minerals in the quantities required.

Home cooking for cats

Beef
Approximately 20–25 per cent protein, and a good source of the major minerals and vitamins A, B$_1$, B$_2$, B$_3$.

As long as it is fit for human consumption, beef can be fed raw, and some cats prefer this. However, proteins can be more easily digested from cooked meat. Do not trim fat; raw or cooked, this is nutritious and cats usually enjoy it. Raw mince (for human consumption) is often a favourite and less expensive than other cuts.

Cheaper cuts of beef are just as nutritious as expensive cuts, so there is no need to spend a lot of money if feeding some beef. In fact, the cheaper cuts will probably be preferred by your cat as they will contain more fat; this makes the entire meal more palatable to a cat. When preparing beef for your own consumption, give your cat the fatty trimmings, which can be fed raw.

Cheese (Cheddar)
About 25 per cent protein and a good source of minerals (high in calcium), contains all vitamins except C.

Cheese (Cottage)
About 17 per cent protein, with less fat than Cheddar, contains the major minerals in smaller quantities except for magnesium (nil), contains vitamins A, B$_1$, B$_2$, B$_3$.

Despite feeding their cats milk foods, many owners

never think of giving their cats raw cheese. It is a good source of most nutrients and many cats will enjoy a small amount grated and added to their food occasionally. Cottage cheese is of benefit given to kittens or overweight cats. (Limit amount of cheese given at first – some cats will eat it until they are sick.)

Chicken

Contains 25–30 per cent protein, phosphorus, calcium and iron and all the vitamins except C and D.

Cats can be fed all leftover parts of chicken (except bone), dark meat, skin, fat, giblets. Chicken liver is particularly well-liked by many cats, either thinly sliced raw or lightly fried. If you buy chicken specifically for your cat, choose a cheaper, old bird and casserole slowly. Serve chopped up or minced with juices poured over. Ensure no bones remain; they become hard and dangerous after cooking and could lodge in your cat's throat.

Egg

Contains 12 per cent protein, and all the major minerals and vitamins except C.

Egg is a useful addition to a kitten or cat's diet. It can be fed on its own for a light meal, or in addition to other food. Egg *white* should *not* be fed raw (see 'Biotin') but can be fed if cooked.

Fish (White)

Contains approximately 25 per cent protein, all the major minerals and vitamins A, B_1, B_2, B_3.

Fish is a 'traditional' food for cats, although it is not a natural food for them as few would bother to catch fish in the wild. Fish should *not* be served raw (see 'Thiamin') but lightly poached. The resulting liquid can be served poured over the fish or can be reserved and poured over cereal.

Bones should be removed and the flaked flesh given to your cat, along with the skin which is a good source of roughage.

Fish (Oily)

Contains approximately 20 per cent protein and all the major minerals. Herring is rich in vitamin D and contains all the other vitamins except E. Mackerel contains vitamins B_1, B_2, B_3, and is particularly rich in vitamin A.

All the comments about white fish also apply to these.

Fish (Tinned: Salmon, Tuna, Sardines)

Tinned salmon contains approximately 20 per cent protein and the major minerals and vitamins except C and E. Pink salmon has less vitamin A than red salmon.

Tinned tuna has 28 per cent protein, calcium, phosphorus and iron with vitamins A, B_1, B_2, and B_3. Salmon and tuna bones should be removed.

Tinned sardines in oil (drained) contain approximately 18 per cent protein, and are rich in minerals and vitamins, except E. Of the three types of tinned fish, they are probably overall the least expensive, most nutritious and are particularly high in calcium.

Lamb

Contains approximately 20–25 per cent protein, all the major minerals and vitamins except C. It is probable that the only lamb fed to most cats will be leftover scraps. Remember that the trimmed fat from chops and joints are enjoyed by cats, raw or cooked, and can help fulfil a cat's energy requirement cheaply.

Milk (Pasteurised, Dried, Evaporated, Cream, Yogurt)

8 oz (1 cup) of milk contains 8 g protein and all the minerals, including 290 mg calcium and 1 mg zinc, plus all

the vitamins. Stored milk loses about one third of its vitamin C content in 12 hours and will also lose a large percentage of its vitamin B_2 content if left in sunlight.

Milk is a 'traditional' food for cats and is a valuable source of nutrients. However, many cats do not like milk and it is not a necessary part of the diet if the diet is otherwise good. In fact, some cats may even be allergic to the lactose in milk. No cat should be given more than one or two tablespoons of milk a day as more than that can lead to diarrhoea. (Fresh water should always be available even if milk is left down.)

If your cat will not drink milk and you would like it to, try giving it reconstituted dried milk, or canned evaporated milk, as many cats will drink this but not bottled milk. Dried milk has the same nutrient content (when reconstituted) as fresh milk, except for the possible loss of B and C vitamins. Evaporated milk has about twice the nutrients of fresh milk but with less vitamins and many cats prefer the taste. Add a little water when giving it to your cat.

Cream is often given to cats as a treat and the fat it contains is a useful energy source. Protein, mineral and vitamin B content is highest in single cream, lowest in the thicker creams, which will have more fat and vitamin A. There is no evidence to suggest that high cholesterol levels have a detrimental effect on a cat.

8 oz of yogurt made from partially skimmed milk contains 8 per cent protein, no magnesium, folic acid or vitamins D or E. Many cats enjoy it and only the plain (unflavoured) variety should be served. It is believed in some quarters that yogurt is a beneficial food to give after a course of antibiotics, in the belief that it will stimulate the growth of intestinal bacteria.

Offal (Liver, kidney, etc.)
Lamb's liver has almost 30 per cent protein and all the

major minerals and vitamins, with a high vitamin A content (75,000 IU per 100 g). For this reason it is dangerous to feed cats any type of liver more than once or twice a week, as it can lead to Hypervitaminosis A (see 'Vitamin A'). Calves' liver has half as much vitamin A as lambs' liver; beef liver contains approximately 53,000 IU per 100 g and chicken liver has approximately 12,000 IU per 100 g. Cats can become addicted to liver and care should be taken not to feed it too regularly. Kidney contains between 25–30 per cent protein, minerals and vitamins A, B_2, B_3, B_6, B_{12} and folic acid. Raw kidney also contains some vitamin B_1 and C.

Heart is less valuable nutritionally, is high in magnesium, and is indigestible in large quantities. Melts (spleen) can cause diarrhoea and is also not recommended as a cat food. Lights (lungs) have almost no nutritional value and should not be fed.

Offal tends to be over-used as a pet food source as it is inexpensive and easy to prepare. This can be dangerous to the cat's health. Care should be taken that offal is fed only in the proportions in which it would be found occurring naturally in prey animals. For example, look at a rabbit (or bird or rat) and note the proportion of flesh to offal. This will indicate the proportions a cat would receive in its natural diet.

Any cooked offal fed should be steamed in foil to retain juices, which should be given to the cat along with the meat. It can also be fed raw if your cat enjoys it that way. Cooking alters the flavour significantly and some cats which do not like cooked offal will enjoy it raw, and vice versa.

Sweetbreads are the thymus gland and contain 26 per cent protein and no vitamins. They do contain solium and are rich in phosphorus and potassium.

Pork

Pork contains between 15–25 per cent protein, minerals and all vitamins except C.

As it is fairly expensive, pork is rarely fed to cats except for leftovers. Pork fat can be a valuable addition to a cat's diet and can be added, chopped, to other food.

Although pork is undoubtedly safer than it once was, always cook pork thoroughly, in case it contains parasites.

Rabbit

Rabbit contains 13 per cent protein, minerals, a trace of vitamin A, as well as vitamins B_1, B_3, B_6 and E.

They should be baked in foil and the retained juices served with the meat, or stewed. Many cats are so fond of rabbit that despite the rabbit's large size, they will catch and kill their own, and it is undoubtedly an item which would occur naturally in their diet.

Turkey

Turkey has 30 per cent protein and vitamins B_1, B_2, B_3 and a trace of A and D.

The meat is rarely fed to cats, except for leftovers; the giblets can be usefully fed to a cat but not more than once a week.

Vegetarian diets

It simply is not possible to feed a cat on a vegetarian diet and for the cat to remain healthy and happy. Because of the cat's *unique* dietary needs, any diet for cats *must* contain food of animal origin.

The cat, unlike most other mammals, is not able to synthesise many of its requirements from other parts of its diet (see under headings in nutritional section).

A cat raised by vegetarian methods may be deficient in

vitamin A, niacin (vitamin B_3), essential fatty acids (EFAs) and taurine (Aminosulphonic acid). There could also be a protein deficiency.

As cats are unable to make vitamin A from vegetables, they must obtain this in the direct form of meat.

Vitamin B_3 is also formed with the help of an amino acid, the same amino acid that a cat uses to produce energy. If a cat requires both vitamin B_3 and energy, the energy requirement will take first priority and no vitamin B_3 will be formed. Offal is an excellent source of this vitamin, so would seem to be essential in the diet, in moderation, of course. (See under separate headings in feeding section.) Animal fats would also appear to be necessary in the diet to supply EFAs.

A cat also needs a large amount of protein for good health. An adult cat needs three times as much as an adult dog, and has an added disadvantage in that it is unable to store proteins in its body.

If protein is not available, the cat's body cuts back the process of using protein to build new cells and tissue.

Taurine can be the most serious deficiency in the vegetarian cat's diet. Other mammals can make their own taurine from two amino acids, cysteine and methionine. As the cat cannot do this adequately, taurine deficiency occurs when it is fed a meatless diet. Taurine is found only in animal products, which include cheese and eggs as well as meat.

Cats are sometimes fed dog food as it is often cheaper but it can be lacking in taurine. This can lead to serious eyesight defects in a cat. Over a long period, it can cause blindness.

Abnormalities have also been found in the retinas of cats fed on a completely vegetarian diet.

This leaves the vegetarian cat-owner with a crisis of conscience; it is simply not possible to raise a cat on vegetarian principles and for the cat to remain healthy throughout its lifespan. Depending on constitution, a kitten living in a strictly vegetarian household would survive for some little time, due to the reserve of nutrition received from its mother's milk, but the kitten would, inevitably, become seriously ill from a variety of deficiencies.

Vegetarians with strong beliefs which extend to their pets' diet, should not consider a cat as a suitable pet for their lifestyle.

Drinks

Milk of human kindness?
You aren't necessarily being kind when you give your cat milk to drink. Milk makes many cats ill.

It is a traditional drink for cats; a hangover from the days when they were fed scraps or had to fend for themselves, but is quite unnecessary nowadays when most cats are receiving well-balanced proprietary diets. No mammals, including cats, need milk once they have been weaned. (See 'Milk', p. 127.)

In fact, your cat is better off drinking nothing but water. Many cats seem to drink very little because they are receiving most of the moisture they need from their food. However a bowl of clean water should always be available, especially if dry food (also called kibble) is fed. There has been criticism of some dry foods (generally those not bought from your vet) which do not supply any dietary moisture, because many cats eating the food do not increase their water intake. In these cases, you can soak the food in water, stock or broth before feeding it to your cat.

Water, water everywhere
An enormous number of cats will not drink water from

their bowls yet regularly quench their thirst in the fish tank (they will eat the fish food too as it is so pleasantly smelly and fishy).

There are probably two reasons why cats will drink from a tank; the water has been sitting for some time during which the chlorinated taste and smell (very apparent to the sensitive cat) has dispersed. The large tank probably also appeals to a deep-rooted instinct in the cat as it would be more like a natural waterhole than a little plastic dish!

So, if your cat won't drink water, you could try supplying it in a fish tank or fish bowl. You don't actually have to add any fish; just a tankful of water would be appreciated.

Or bottle tapwater for a day or two before pouring it into your cat's dish – that will be enough time for the chlorine to disperse. Or, if you really want to spoil your cat, give it bottled spring water (still water, not carbonated – there is no such thing as a Perrier puss).

Some cats enjoy water to which a little honey has been added. For a cat which really will not drink, you could try making a 'consommé' by boiling up a few meaty scraps or bones in water and pouring the strained, cooled liquid into your cat's bowl.

One thing fascinates many owners: they have noticed that their cat will tap the surface of the water in its bowl before drinking. Because mythology has it that cats are cussed creatures, they wonder if their cat is doing this for the pleasure of trampling wet footprints over the kitchen floor. Like most cat stories, this too, is pure myth. A cat will tap the water in its bowl to make it move, so that it can judge from the movement how far away the water is – and not get its nose wet when drinking.

Moggy Miscellany

Missing cats

Missing – not strayed

Tens of thousands of cats go missing every year in the United Kingdom. Very few of them will have strayed.

It is very rare for a cat to stray. If a cat is missing it will usually be lost, trapped, injured or killed, or stolen. In a few rare cases, the cat will have packed its bags and moved in with a neighbour if it has taken a dislike to a new family addition such as another pet, or to a family member. It won't usually move far and you'll know where it is.

If your cat is missing, don't forget to search your own home thoroughly first. Your cat may just be sleeping comfortably in the airing-cupboard.

It's helpful to know your cat is missing before too much time has elapsed. If possible, have 'check-points' throughout the day at regular times. This is easier if your cat doesn't use a cat flap, for you will be letting it in and out and will always know whether it is indoors or not.

Many cats go missing at weekends in early spring. This is the time gardeners get to work, opening sheds and green-houses which have been locked since autumn. While they work in their gardens, the doors are left open. Curious cats explore the sheds, then hear the gardener return. Most will hide in the shed and the gardener, not knowing they are there, relocks the shed, trapping them inside.

So if the weather has been fine for the first time in weeks or months and your cat goes missing, start your search of garden sheds and similar outbuildings. It helps if you know your cat's territory, so you can restrict your search to that area. Enlist the help of neighbours and ask them to search any sheds and outhouses. It is best if you can accompany them; your cat may respond to your calling but hide again if a stranger calls.

One Bournemouth couple toured the streets whistling 'Danny Boy' – their missing cat's favourite song. He rushed out to greet them in response to the tune!

Has a neighbour had a delivery made or has a neighbour moved house? When delivery lorries are left open, a cat will explore and may be shut up when the driver returns. It will then usually run away once the door is opened again, which may be several hundred miles from your home. So make enquiries among your neighbours and contact any delivery firms who may be involved. Remember to ask, not only the lorry's final destination, but if any stops were made en route.

A missing cat may have been injured, either deliberately or by traffic. If not caught and taken to a vet, a cat will crawl away and hide while it recovers. When it feels better, it will return home if it can. So if you know your cat's territory, look in any of the hiding places you know within it. An injured cat may not respond to its owner's call, so you will have to find it.

If your cat has been stolen, there is little likelihood you will get it back. Moggy owners often feel secure from theft, thinking that the only cats which are stolen are valuable pedigrees. In fact, stolen pedigree cats are relatively worthless without their pedigree papers; they cannot be resold and any offspring cannot be registered and sold as pedigrees.

Almost all cats which are stolen are moggies. Many are stolen for their fur which is taken abroad and becomes pelts used to 'ward off rheumatism' or as parts of coats. Cats of all colours are stolen and it is common to discover that a number of cats of one coat colour disappear from one area at the same time. It would seem they are stolen to order.

You can prevent this theft by ensuring your cat is kept indoors each night from dusk onwards. (Cats don't mind this if they become used to being indoors at night from kittenhood. If your cat is used to an outdoor nightlife, it can still be converted as long as you provide it with all the comforts it needs, a good meal, a comfortable bed and a litter tray, although you may have to listen to a lot of indignant complaints for several nights.)

If your cat is not particularly friendly towards strangers, it is less likely to be stolen. It will run away from thieves instead of going to greet them. So it is not always a good idea to encourage your cat to be friendly towards others.

What to do before your cat goes missing
The time to make your preparations to find a missing cat is *before* it goes missing.

Can you describe your cat accurately? You should sit down one day with your cat and jot down a complete description. This is much easier when your cat is beside you than when you are upset because it is missing.

Do you have a clear photograph of your cat? If not, take one and keep it in a safe place with your written description and the negative. It will be invaluable if you have to advertise to find your pet.

Are you able to offer a reward? This is often a great incentive for local children, in particular, to spend time looking for a missing pet. If children are helping you in your search, do ensure they are careful of their own safety and that they don't go into isolated or wooded areas alone. Tell them if they find your pet, and it is injured, that they should not approach it but should immediately report the cat's whereabouts to you.

If you have taken out pet health insurance for your cat,

many schemes include insurance coverage in the event of loss or theft and the insurance company will pay the reward for you. Check your policy and keep the details with your cat's photograph and description.

Does your cat wear a collar and identity disc? These are available from all pet stores. Although many owners are loath to collar their cats in case they are trapped by them, they can help identify a found pet. There are pet registries which provide identity discs engraved with an individual number which will identify a pet, along with the bureau's telephone number. The finder contacts the bureau and the owner can be told their pet has been found.

One registry allocates an individual number to a pet which is stored on computer. The number is also tattooed inside the pet's ear, under anaesthetic. It is said to be painless and recommended to be carried out at the same time as another surgical procedure, for example neutering.

The newest idea to identify lost pets is a microchip implant. It is encased in a tiny glass capsule, just 2 milli-metres in diameter and injected into a muscle under local anaesthetic. The implant remains for the rest of the animal's life and its 10-digit code can be 'read' by a handwand to identify the pet.

What to do when your cat goes missing

First, speak to all your neighbours or put photocopied notes through their letterboxes. Ask them to check any sheds or buildings which were open when your cat disappeared. Also ask them if any vans or lorries were delivering anything to them that day.

Make up small posters or cards, using your cat's photo and description, and place these in local shop windows. Pet store staff are usually particularly helpful, and someone who finds a cat may inform their local pet store.

Place a large poster in the window of your home; passers-by may have seen your cat. A ten-year-old computer buff who lost his cat made up computer pictures of his missing pet and distributed them to his neighbours.

Contact your local police station. Although the police are not obliged to keep records of lost and found cats, many officers can be very helpful.

Telephone all the vets in the vicinity, not just your own vet. Most people, if they find an injured cat, will take it to their own vet, who might not be the nearest. Most vets keep a 'lost and found' book as a service to their clients.

Contact all the welfare organisations in your area; not just the big ones. Often there is a local person who keeps records of missing pets. Keep in touch with them and telephone them several times a week. Often they can be too busy to telephone you. If they are a large organisation with many cats, visit their premises. It is possible your cat may not be recognised from your description.

In case your cat has been killed by traffic, contact your local authority road-cleaning department. Many keep records of pets found on the roads. Also ask your council if strays are being trapped in the area. If you live near a railway line, contact your local station. Railway lines are inspected frequently and workmen often report any pets they have found. If you live in a rural area, ask farmers if they are setting traps.

Many local radio stations will broadcast appeals for missing pets, so get in touch with them too.

Advertise in the 'Lost and Found' section of your local newspaper. Some newspapers provide this service free of charge and with some there is a small charge. Only around one in five missing cats are advertised in newspapers, possibly because of the time delay before the newspaper is printed; most owners think they will get their cats back before then. This is not always true, so it is a good idea to advertise.

If you have moved home, get in touch with the occupant at your old address. Your cat may have moved back there.

Don't give up hope if your cat is missing. There are many recorded cases of cats turning up, safe and well, on their owner's doorstep several months or even years after going missing.

In several cases, psychics have been brought in by worried owners although I have never heard of a case where they have actually found the cat concerned.

Cats and divorce

Some of the most bitterly contested divorce battles have been over who gets custody of the cat! In a case in Britain, the husband took the cat, so his estranged wife kidnapped the family car – and refused to hand it back until she was given the cat in exchange. In another, more serious case, a husband was fatally knifed in a quarrel over the custody of the family cats.

Divorce is one of the most stressful experiences human beings can live through. Even if the divorce is relatively amicable there is a period of great tension and trauma which can last for a number of years.

Cats are affected by the trauma of divorce too, in a number of ways. First, a person they probably loved disappears from their lives (and of course this can also be the case if a member of the family dies). Second, they are aware – and disturbed by – the tensions felt by the remaining partner. Third, they may lose the companionship of another cat if they live in a multi-cat household which is split up.

Cats are creatures of habit. They hate having any part of

their lifestyles changed unless they decide to change it themselves. A person leaving their life is a major change and a cat may feel stressed by this change alone. The older a cat is, the more vulnerable it is to stress. An entire cat is even less able to cope with stress than a neutered cat.

Cats often have a deep emotional bond with their owners. If an owner is unhappy, the cat will be aware of this. Even if voices are not raised, cats can pick up distress signals from their owner's body language and tone of voice.

Cats can be wonderful companions to someone left alone after a divorce but they have their needs too. If you can try to overcome your anxieties, it will be easier for your cat too. Although it is not always easy when there are many extra calls on your time, try to give it extra love and attention. Cuddles and conversation will make you both feel better. Playing with your cat is a great stress reliever for you both and a few minutes spent in this way daily will help. And, if you pour yourself a gin and tonic to help you relax, give your cat a sprinkle of catnip to help *it* relax.

The stress of the divorce may result in behavioural problems in your cat, such as soiling in the house, at a time when you are least able to cope with this. (See 'Problem Pages', p. 196.) Keeping your cat as happy and secure as possible will minimise this possibility and result in many benefits for you both.

Divorcing couples should try to give thought to the welfare of their cat at the time they discuss the split of the family assets. If there is one cat, which partner would *it* choose to live with? If there is more than one cat, are they close companions or do they simply tolerate one another? If they are close, splitting them up will make both cats feel even more insecure and unhappy. If they are cats which just tolerate one another, they might be happier living apart.

At least one couple who divorced and now cannot stand the sight of one another get together once a year so that their pining cats can be reunited with one another!

Cats and babies

One of the many cat myths is that cats steal a baby's breath. They don't – they have plenty of their own. The idea may have started because cats have been seen cuddled up to babies. The reason they do this is the same reason they do many things; they like sleeping in a warm place.

Women should take additional hygiene precautions while pregnant. An infection called Toxoplasmosis poses a risk to the foetus if a cat is infected and a pregnant owner does not wash her hands after cleaning out the cat's litter tray. Risk can be avoided by wearing rubber gloves when cleaning out a tray, or asking someone else to do it. Toxoplasmosis need not be a cause for worry as long as sensible hygiene precautions are taken.

If a baby is soon to arrive in your household, should you be concerned about how the two will get on? The answer is no – cats and babies can cohabit peacefully and safely when the parents deal with both sensibly.

Cats need to know everything about their environment for their own safety and peace of mind. So don't expect to redecorate the baby's room without the cat being curious to see it. Let it into the room some weeks before the baby arrives so that it can accustom itself to the new smells. Similarly, when the baby arrives, when its clothing needs to be washed, you can allow your cat to sniff it. Cats learn a great deal about their environment by smell. After your cat has been allowed to sniff out the baby's room, it will probably show no further interest in it and can then be barred from the room.

Remember that your cat may feel stressed by the new arrival if it means that it no longer receives as much attention, or if its routine is drastically changed. Obviously, baby comes first and it is a busy time but try to spend time with your cat too so that it doesn't feel left out. Stress can lead to behavioural problems (see 'Problem Pages', p. 192), but, if they do occur, they should be temporary, and will cease when the cat gets used to having a new member of the family around.

If you do have to make changes such as moving your cat's bed, bowls or litter tray, try to make them some months before the baby arrives, to give your cat time to get used to them.

If your cat tries to investigate the baby as soon as it arrives home, don't scold but allow it to do so under supervision. Some cats will completely ignore the newcomer but others will want to have a look. Don't worry that your cat might injure the baby; I've never heard of this happening and most cats are surprisingly gentle and tolerant of babies, not even complaining when their fur is pulled.

You can keep the door to the baby's room closed while it is asleep to keep your cat out. Whether allowed into the room or not, don't allow your cat to sleep in the baby's cot. It's simple to make a screen cover for the cot to keep the cat out, if you feel it is necessary.

When baby reaches the crawling stage, it is vital that you ensure your cat continues to be regularly wormed and flea treatments are carried out. If a young child swallows an infected flea which has been left on the carpet, it could end up with tapeworms. This should not be a problem if preventative treatment against worms and fleas is carried out regularly.

In years to come, your cat will be friend and companion to your child. It is known that children turn to their pets for comfort, which is particularly important if both parents work or the family moves house frequently. Children who grow up with animals find them a source of comfort and friendship and it helps them develop a sense of responsibility and a more caring attitude to others.

Cats and allergies

The loose fur you remove from your cat by combing it can help people who have an allergic reaction to cats to live with them. Densensitising injections for cat allergy are available (although they are not suitable for everyone) and the raw material is made from cat combings!

Cat allergies may be caused by several different allergens: it may be a cat's fur, the dander on its skin or its saliva. This is why it is so difficult to effectively help some allergy sufferers. Unfortunately, for someone suffering a serious allergy there is only one remedy – don't keep a cat.

A cat lover who is unable to keep a cat because of allergy might consider sponsoring a cat at a rescue centre. For a monthly fee, the sponsored cat becomes 'theirs' but continues to live at the shelter. Many shelters will supply photographs and progress reports of the cat to sponsors. Sponsored cats are usually animals which are difficult to re-house because of age, disability, or some other reason.

In some cases of cat allergy, desensitising injections are effective and, for those with a very mild allergy, there are a number of steps you can take to minimise the problem.

First, cats should be groomed daily to reduce the amount of fur shed. If a sufferer can persuade someone else to do this for them, that's even better! Keeping a cat's coat in good condition can help too, so add a coat conditioner to its food. If a cat doesn't object to being bathed, regular bathing will help remove loose fur and dander. Use a shampoo specifically formulated for cats, not a dandruff shampoo for humans which could be toxic for the cat.

Other allergens in the environment may add to a sufferer's discomfort, so smooth, washable surfaces in the home are beneficial. Linoleum or wood flooring is better than carpets, which, if used, should be thoroughly vacuumed frequently. Blinds are better than curtains, which can collect dust and hairs. When dusting, a damp cloth is better than a dry duster at collecting debris.

An air purifier can be of enormous benefit to allergy sufferers as long as it is the type which does not produce ozone, which can be another allergy irritant. A commercial air purifier for use in shops or offices will be much more effective than a 'home-size' one.

Litter trays should be emptied carefully and a sufferer might find it helps to wear a dust mask such as do-it-yourself shops stock. The type of litter used should be chosen for its low-dust qualities.

It isn't only humans who suffer from allergies – cats can too. It is quite possible for them to be allergic to their litter and here too, a dust-free, additive-free litter will help. Some asthmatic cats have benefited when their litter has been changed from the clay type to a wood-based litter.

A cat can be allergic to its food – even a manufactured cat food which has no ill effect on most other cats. It may be an additive which is at fault, or it may be the meat used. Some cats are allergic to red meat! These cats, under veterinary supervision, are placed on diets of fish and chicken.

Quite a few cats are allergic to the lactose in milk and should only be given water to drink.

Cats can have allergic reactions to many things in their environment such as plastic bowls, household cleansers, fleas, pollen and cigarette smoke, which may manifest themselves as coughs, rashes, bald spots, sickness, diarrhoea or in a number of other ways. If you suspect that your cat's illness might be due to an allergy, consult with your vet until the source is found.

At least no one has yet reported a case of a cat suffering an allergic reaction to humans!

Cats in danger

It's fortunate that cats have nine lives as this world holds so many dangers for them.

The most innocuous-seeming substances can kill a cat or make it extremely ill. These include everyday items such as aspirin and paracetamol, disinfectants and antiseptics based on Phenol (carbolic acid) and Cresol (which include Dettol, TCP and Jeyes Fluid), many dog medications, anti-freeze, tranquillisers and sleeping tablets prescribed for their owners, tobacco, prepared cooked meats containing benzoic acid, chocolate and many household and garden plants.

Among those plants which are toxic to cats are dieffenbachias, poinsettias, castor oil plants, daffodils, crocuses, hyacinths, iris, lily-of-the-valley, chrysanthemums, philodendrons, yew, winter cherry, oleander, Jerusalem cherry, laurel, azaleas, rhododendrons, larkspur, foxglove, lupins, laburnum, broom and monkshood. Of course, many cats live in homes with many of these plants without suffering ill effects because they are not silly enough to eat them. But if you do have a choice between a poisonous and non-poisonous plant, choose the latter.

Mistletoe is also toxic to cats, and the needles from pine Christmas trees can cause problems if swallowed. Imitation trees are better in a catty household and are more durable if knocked over. Decorate your tree when your cat isn't in the room: if it sees the baubles swinging it will want to play with them and this becomes a regular game. Never place glass baubles on your tree as these shatter easily. Use flex protectors over Christmas tree light flex if your cat chews wires.

Shampoos made for humans, especially dandruff shampoos, should never be used on cats. And some household cleansers can make a cat ill if it walks on a newly-cleaned surface, then licks wet paws. Household bleach is the safest surface and floor cleaner but all surfaces should be dry before a cat is allowed into the room.

Treatments to make carpets waterproof can irritate your cat's eyes and woodworm treatments can be lethal. Dieldrin is used to treat affected timbers and there are many recorded cases of Dieldrin poisoning in cats, even if the cats have not moved into the treated home until several weeks afterwards and even when carpets have been replaced over the wooden floors. Homes treated with spirit-based Dieldrin preparations become safe before those treated with an oil-based Dieldrin product. Some owners place their cats in catteries for several weeks if woodworm treatment has recently been carried out. Ideally, they should be rehoused elsewhere for five or six weeks.

The garden is a particularly dangerous place for a cat. Insecticides should be used with care when cats use a garden. The safest are pyrethrum and derris dust, although cats should still be kept away from treated areas.

Weedkillers can cause problems too; although many are stated to be safe to pets once the product has been applied and has dried, they can still be active next morning when dew or rain has moistened them. If you use weedkillers, spread them late at night and do not allow your cat out again until after the sun has risen and dried the ground thoroughly.

The safest way to weed when cats are around is to pull the weeds out by hand. Alternatively, sprinkle weeds with common salt; it is cheap, effective and safe.

Slug pellets are very attractive to cats and are toxic. If you use them, place them underneath an upended flowerpot, weighted down with stones. A safer method of disposing of slugs and snails is to place shallow lids or saucers containing beer in the garden. Slugs love beer; they drink it, fall in and drown, so at least they die happy.

Unsterilised bonemeal and fertilisers are two more garden hazards for cats. Stone them in lidded containers rather than sacks which may split or spill their contents.

Use great care if creosoting a fence as creosote contains a high concentration of phenol. Creosote is corrosive and burns the affected areas. Cats will try to lick it off and so will swallow corrosive chemical. Swarfega (used by mechanics as a hand cleanser) will wash creosote from your cat's fur or paws but then must be thoroughly rinsed out. Washing-up liquid in water will remove creosote, but not quite as effectively. If any creosote has been swallowed, give your cat milk to neutralise the acid effects and immediately call your vet.

Symptoms of poisoning include vomiting, diarrhoea, fits and a staggering gait. A cat which has been poisoned should be left in a secure, dark place while you immediately telephone your vet. If you know what has caused the problem, inform your vet over the telephone so that antidotes can be prepared without delay. Containers should be scrutinised so that the poisonous substance can be identified.

Dangers around the home include wool and string, which cats should never be allowed to play with on their own. Because cats have rough, rasping tongues, they are unable to spit out string or wool once it gets into their mouths and have to swallow it. This can become entangled in the intestines and, if so, an immediate operation will be necessary to save the cat's life.

A similar effect occurs when a cat swallows cotton threaded through a sewing-needle. Once the cotton is in its mouth, it has to swallow it, needle and all. Never leave a needle threaded – it is potentially lethal.

A cat or kitten can be badly burned or killed by chewing electrical flexes. Kittens are inclined to chew flexes when they are teething. Cover flex with flex protectors or remove all plugs from sockets when you are not in the room.

Kittens are also in danger from lavatories! They frequently jump on to the seat and, if they fall into the bowl, are unable to get out again. Always close the cover when kittens are around. Do not leave cleansers in the bowl without closing the lid either. Lots of cats drink out of the toilet bowl.

Cats can be badly burned when they jump on to cookers when the hotplates have not cooled down. Keep your cat out of the kitchen or train it to keep away from the cooker from an early age.

Many cats are killed when washing-machines and dish-washers are turned on with them inside. Always close the door, then check your cat or cats' whereabouts before switching on. One cat was trapped in a refrigerator for twelve hours, pronounced dead by a vet, yet got up and walked away seven hours later!

Do be careful that you don't allow non-stick pans to burn dry. The fumes they give off can kill a cat.

Many cats are killed or injured in falls from windows. Never open a window more than an inch or two because a cat, stalking an insect or catching sight of a bird, will leap after it through a window, no matter how high. Or a cat sleeping on a windowsill may just roll off.

Cats have survived some remarkable falls: 18 storeys onto a hard concrete surface, 20 storeys on to shrubbery and 28 storeys on to an awning. However, cats involved in much shorter falls have been killed. One five-month-old kitten fell from the lid of an upright piano on to the keyboard – breaking its neck. It is thought the reason for this is that falling from a greater height gives the cat time to adopt an aerodynamic position, spreading out its limbs to take full advantage of the cushion of air beneath.

In effect, given time to get into position, cats can fly!

Cats on holiday

Cat-sitting

Have you ever thought of taking your cat on holiday with you?

If you are not travelling to a country where rabies is endemic (and you are not restricted by quarantine laws), and your cat has a suitable temperament and does not mind travelling and new places, it could be the solution of a recurring problem. Many people take their cats on holiday with them, camping, caravanning, or staying in hotels. Many hotels and guest houses will now accept pets (although the pets they usually expect are dogs) and books are now published which list all hotels, guest houses and caravan parks where pets are welcome. Ensure you take with you a good supply of your cat's food, in case it is not immediately available locally, its litter tray and a good supply of litter (litter always runs out on the day the local shops are closed), and, if your cat is a confirmed stropper of furniture, its scratching post.

There are other holiday alternatives which you may not have considered. Petsitters advertise their services in local newspapers. They will visit your home once or twice a day, caring for your pets (and watering your plants) at a fee per visit. There are also homesitting agencies which will arrange for someone to live full-time in your home while you are away and look after it and your pets. This service, as you might expect, is fairly expensive.

You can take advantage of a similar service which not only will cost you nothing – but you get a free holiday thrown in. Home exchange agencies will assist you in exchanging your home with that of another homeowner. The exchangee will look after your home and pets while you look after theirs. However, my own experience of this form of home exchange is that many people were very interested in staying in my seaside house and less interested in looking after my cats! To solve this problem, at least one specialist agency has started up which arranges exchanges among pet-owners only.

The ideal arrangement, when possible, is to have a reliable neighbour come in several times a day to feed and look after your cat. If they charge a fee for this service it is usually reasonable and your cat benefits because it is able to stay in familiar surroundings with visits from someone it knows.

But the most often taken option is placing the cat in a holiday home of their own – a boarding cattery.

Choosing a cattery
The best time to book your cat into a cattery for a summer holiday is January! The best catteries, like the best summer holidays, become fully booked soon after Christmas.

Find cattery addresses by looking in your *Yellow Pages* or from a book listing boarding catteries. Even if you find a cattery recommended in a book, visit it yourself before booking and ask to see *all* around it. Reputable cattery owners will expect this, so if an owner refuses to let you see all over the premises, go elsewhere. There are one or two catteries which have modern, hygienic accommodation in full view and cramped, unhygienic accommodation hidden at the back, where most of the cats stay.

If the cattery is of the type which has numbers of pens

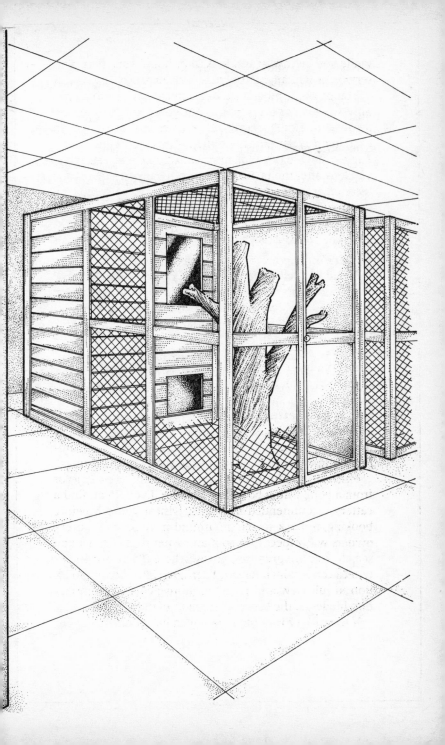

piled one on top of the other, go elsewhere. There is a very high risk of infection at this type of cattery. Cats should be kept well separated. Ideally they should have chalets or houses with their own individual runs with solid floors which can be easily disinfected (not grass). There should be about a metre between each run or an impermeable 'sneeze barrier' between, so if an infected cat sneezes, it doesn't do so over your cat and pass on any infection.

Chalets should have individual, safe heating, in case of cold weather. The cat should have plenty of space to roam around and a comfortable shelf to sleep on as well as a good view of what is around it. A cat can become very bored and unhappy if it doesn't have a good view. There should be two sets of doors to be negotiated before entering the run so, if a cat gets out of its accommodation, it is unable to escape. If dogs are boarded at the same location, they should be well out of sight and smell of the cats.

Check that accommodation, feeding bowls and litter trays are kept clean and that there are no bad smells. Cats already boarding there should look content. Staff should show interest in your cat's requirements. Accommodation should be thoroughly sterilised between boarders.

Check what the cats are fed. If it is a food your cat does not like or which upsets it, ensure that the staff are willing to feed it on an individual basis. Some catteries will ask that you bag and label food if you require a specific diet for your cat; they may even charge you extra because this gives them extra work!

All reputable catteries will insist that your cat's inoculations are up to date before they will accept it. Do not use a cattery where this is not insisted upon.

And, when packing your suitcases, do not forget to pack your cat's bag too. It will be much happier in its new surroundings with a familiar-smelling blanket and a few favourite toys.

Moggy Maintenance

Neutering and spaying

Neutering and spaying have been called 'a cat having its squeak taken out'!

In a male cat, neutering means castration at any time from around four months to nine months of age. Humans, especially men, wince at the word castration. Many see it in human terms and some insist that their cats remain entire. Entire tomcats have a much shorter life expectancy than a neutered male, they run up bigger vet's bills as they get into more fights (usually over females), they disappear for days at a time to find females in season, often coming back thin and injured, they annoy the neighbours with their noise and smell, and they are not very pleasant to have around, as they spray their pungent urine everywhere.

Neutered males have fewer fights and fewer injuries, they do not wander off, they are much less likely to spray indoors, they do not act over-aggressively to neighbourhood cats, and they are a delight to have around. They don't become fat and sluggish because of the operation and, most importantly, they don't miss what they haven't got. They are not producing the male hormone testosterone once they are neutered so they don't know what sex is or show any interest in it. Their supposed sexual frustration is a purely human concept!

The operation is a minor one and many male cats are running around half an hour after returning from the vet's, demanding the breakfast they didn't have! (A cat should not be fed on the day surgery is due to be carried out.) Your vet will advise you of the best time to have your male cat neutered, or your female spayed.

Spaying entails removal of the ovaries and womb (uterus) of the female between the ages of four to nine months. Although this is a more complicated operation than neutering, a cat does not need the long convalescent period that a human who has had a hysterectomy requires. Within twenty-four hours, a spayed female will be up and around, none the worse for the operation.

There are absolutely no health benefits in allowing a cat to have one litter before spaying. In fact, the opposite is the case; the cat is put through the frightening and painful birth experience with the ever-present risk of complications (some cats are unable to give birth naturally, and have to have a Caesarian operation which is traumatic for the cat and expensive for the owner).

The resulting kittens add to the total of moggies which need to find homes each year and often do not. And don't expect the local rescue centre to take them off your hands if you can't find homes for them; in the summer months rescue centres are always overfull, with a long list of cats and kittens waiting to get in.

I estimate that there are 250,000 unwanted cats and kittens arriving in rescue centres each year in the United Kingdom alone; tens of thousands of which are put down as no homes are available for them. Your cat's kittens either become part of that statistic or they prevent another kitten from finding a home.

Some owners allow their cats to become pregnant because they would like a kitten but feel their cat would not accept a strange kitten joining the household. Cats will usually accept strange kittens quite readily. However, a cat which has kittens expects them to move on as they mature; very often a cat will actively dislike her offspring if they remain with her beyond the age of three months.

Kittens adore their mother's milk and may continue to feed from her long after they should have been weaned, leaving your cat run down and tired.

Also, a cat will usually defer to her kittens at mealtimes; this can continue throughout her life, long after she has forgotten the reason for it. A cat living with one of her offspring should always be carefully monitored to ensure she is receiving enough food.

Some owners want to mate their moggy females with a pedigree male, because they believe their cat has some particular quality they wish to carry on. Mating a moggy with a pedigree cat is virtually impossible as no reputable breeder will allow it. They would be drummed out of their cat clubs and organisations for producing crossbreeds. If you find someone who will permit it, it is almost certain they will be a 'back-street' unknowledgeable breeder and you will be exposing your cat to illness and disease.

Spaying and neutering are the kindest cuts of all.

When a kitten living in a Brighton pub was to be neutered, the regulars had a 'going away' party for him. The pub is called Nobles!

Yearly vaccinations

Cat 'flu is the common name for a number of viruses which can produce respiratory infections. It is a misleading name because, in humans, influenza is rarely serious. In cats, influenza is often fatal.

Kittens are protected for the first two months or so of life by antibodies from their mother but then need a vaccination to protect them from cat 'flu.

The first vaccination is given at about nine weeks with a second vaccination three to four weeks later. Your kitten is not fully protected until about a week after the second vaccination and should be kept indoors until then. Yearly boosters are necessary to continue protection.

Moggies appear to be less susceptible to cat 'flu than pedigree cats. In an outbreak in a cattery, 80 per cent of Siamese were affected, compared to 50 per cent of moggies. Nevertheless, every caring owner will ensure their cat is regularly vaccinated. (See also 'Moggy Medicine', p. 172.)

Feline Enteritis is another infectious, and often fatal, disease of cats. It can be prevented by vaccination which is combined with the cat 'flu vaccine.

Rarely, a cat will have a bad reaction to the vaccine. One cat became very ill six weeks after its first vaccination, then unwell again four weeks after its booster the following year, then again two weeks after its booster the year after. The cat recovered each time, but the owner had not connected the illness with the vaccinations due to the time lapse between. This is one of the few cats which is no longer vaccinated.

Reputable catteries will not admit cats without up-to-date certificates of vaccination; neither will they be allowed to enter a cat show.

Although the vaccinations add a few pounds a year to the cost of keeping a cat, it is a great deal less than paying for treatment for an ill cat; and an infected cat might not survive.

The United Kingdom, Australia, New Zealand, Hawaii and Scandinavia (apart from Finland) are fortunate in that they are currently free from rabies. In other parts of the world, cats and other pets are vaccinated to protect them from the disease. Vaccination can be started at three months of age, after which annual boosters are given.

Worms

Intestinal worms are such successful parasites that symptoms can be difficult to spot, yet they do an excellent job of robbing their host of nourishment. This quality was taken full advantage of in Edwardian England, when society beauties would swallow tapeworms, under medical supervision, to enable them to eat generous meals without putting on weight.

Signs of worm infestation in the cat can include occasional diarrhoea or vomiting, with segments of worms sometimes visible. Cats and kittens may lose weight, yet have a pot belly, look out of condition, become restless, cough, and the third eyelid may show.

If harbouring tapeworms, small segments, looking like brownish grains of rice, may be visible around the cat's bottom or, having dropped off, in the cat's bed. These segments may still be wriggling!

When the worm infestation is severe, the cat may be off its food. Occasionally, intestinal blockage can occur in untreated young kittens which can be life-threatening. Kittens can be born infected with worms or can become infected via their mother's milk. Cats become infected by eating prey whose bodies contain encysted larvae, which develop into worms if swallowed by a cat, or by swallowing a flea with worm eggs in its system.

All cats and kittens should be wormed regularly, whether or not symptoms are present. Your vet will give advice on the frequency of dosage for any preparations purchased from the veterinary surgery. Pet stores also sell worming preparations and manufacturer's instructions should be adhered to rigidly.

Overdosage, especially in a kitten, can be fatal. Cats should always be given worming preparations specifically formulated for cats; those made for dogs can be toxic to cats. And worming preparations should not be given within days of flea treatments; used together, the two treatments can prove toxic.

There are different types of worms and they require

different products for their treatment. A roundworm preparation, for example, will be ineffective against tapeworms. Preparations are available which are effective against both.

Roundworms are cylindrical and can be up to 10 centimetres long. Although, rarely, dog roundworms (*Toxocara canis*) can be transmitted to humans, causing serious health problems, there is no evidence that infection with the cat roundworm (*Toxocara cati*) causes any human illness.

Hookworms are a type of roundworm which can penetrate intestinal membranes and feed on the cat's blood. This can cause weakness and anaemia.

Tapeworms have long, segmented bodies and require different preparations for treatment than do roundworms. They can cause anaemia and occasional digestive upsets.

Lungworms can cause coughing and, if untreated, can lead to pneumonia. You may not have heard of lungworms, but 9 per cent of cats in a Scottish sample were found to be infected with them. Veterinary advice should be sought if lungworms are suspected.

Many worm preparations are now 'palatable'. That is, they will be eaten by cats as if they were treats. But cats are too clever to eat conventional worm preparations mixed up in their food, so the tablets have to be administered by the owner. Hold your cat gently between your knees, facing away from you (having first wrapped its body in a towel if it is a scratcher). Tip its head back gently and drop the pill as far back as you can in the throat. Hold its mouth closed, without covering the nose, while you gently stroke under its chin, or blow on its nose. Either action will make it swallow. Alternatively, cover the pill with cream cheese and you will find that your cat will gobble it up. It will love the cheese and, because it's so sticky, it can't spit it out.

Some worm preparations are in the form of granules which can be chilled in the fridge to lessen the taste then mixed with food. Herbalists swear by garlic, usually given in capsule form, as an intestinal cleanser reputed to keep cats free from worms. Vets who use homoeopathic remedies will provide *Cina* or *Santonin* for use against roundworms and pomegranate to expel tapeworms.

Fleas

Spray away

Fleas are now a year-round, rather than seasonal problem.

The comfortable surroundings that most of us enjoy, such as central heating and wall-to-wall carpeting, are good news for fleas too as flea eggs will hatch in the relatively undisturbed surroundings of the edges of carpets, encouraged by the warmth of our homes.

Cat fleas spend most of their lives on their feline host, and in one month a flea can lay 300 eggs, of which around 250 will hatch. As a badly-infested cat may have 50 fleas, if untreated, at the end of one month it can be responsible for 12,500 fleas! It's no wonder that professional exterminators have to be called in if the situation is allowed to get out of hand.

Cat fleas will bite humans too, which is embarrassing as well as unhygienic, but they will not live on humans, finding cats much tastier. However, some diseases can be transmitted to humans bitten by an infected cat flea. In the Western United States, plague is still found among rodents. A hunting cat can pick up infected fleas from their prey which, if they bite a human, can infect them with bubonic plague!

If you brush or comb your cat at least once a week, always check for the presence of fleas. You may actually see a flea, a tiny reddish-brown insect, but you are more likely to discover their presence by their droppings; blackish specks in the fur. These turn red when wetted because fleas live on blood, some of which is passed undigested in their faeces. Check particularly under the chin, around the ears and at the base of the tail; these are the fleas' favourite areas. If you wait until you see your cat scratching, there will already be a large number of fleas present.

Fleas must be treated promptly because they feed on a cat's blood, can transmit disease and cause scratching during which a cat can injure itself. A cat may also develop an allergic reaction to flea bites, causing eczema, and become infected with tapeworms, if it swallows an infected flea. Cats can become debilitated if heavily infested and become vulnerable to disease.

But, because the cat's environment may be harbouring unhatched eggs, just treating your cat will be ultimately ineffective. Newly hatched fleas will still hop on to your cat even after you have rid it of fleas, and the cycle will start again. The home must be treated when your cat is treated, using products specifically formulated for that purpose.

Most environment treatments are in the form of insecticidal sprays or powders which work by killing the insect. These are for spraying around the home only, and should never be used on a cat. Always follow directions printed on these, and any other flea preparations extremely carefully. One of the newer sprays utilises methoprene, which inhibits the development of the flea larvae, preventing them from becoming adults. It is quite safe for use around cats as its effects are specific to insects.

Treatments for use on the cat's fur are usually in the form of sprays or powders. Again, these should be used with extreme care, following directions minutely.

Different types of flea product should not be used together as, combined, they can be extremely toxic.

Organophosphates have been rated most efficient by United States vets and these will have phosphate – or phospho – in their ingredients list. Carbamates act in a similar manner but degrade more rapidly. Pyrethrum is slightly less effective, although possibly safer than some other products. Chlorinated hydrocarbons are effective and long-lasting. As always, veterinary advice in the choice of flea products is useful. Flea products available from vets are usually more effective than those from pet stores or supermarkets.

When spraying your cat, or the environment, always remove food and water bowls from the room – and your fish tank, if you have one. These sprays can kill fish as well as fleas.

Spray your cat out of doors, if you can, in a short burst along its back and stomach. You do not have to spray every inch of the cat's fur for the product to be effective. Wear rubber gloves, especially if you have to spray several cats and spray downwind so neither you nor your cat inhales the spray.

Don't spray your cat within several days of worming it as, combined, these treatments can be toxic. Always seek veterinary advice if young kittens have fleas, as many products suitable for adult cats are dangerous for kittens.

It always has to be borne in mind that insecticides are toxic – they have to be to kill fleas – and they can be toxic to cats and humans if not used properly. Always follow directions and never overdose. More is *not* better where flea sprays are concerned.

In fact, some flea treatment products may cause problems even when used according to directions. The United States Environmental Protection Agency has, in recent months, issued a warning that insecticides containing dichlorvos (an organophosphate found in some flea treatments, flea collars, and worming products) has been linked to cancer in humans and animals, exposed long-term to it. The United States Consumers' Union point out that, even though the product will now undergo the EPA's Special Review procedure to determine whether the product should remain on the market, this could take many years, and recommend that pet owners should avoid using dichlorvos in the meantime.

Cats know you are spraying them with toxic chemicals — that is why they always run away when the flea spray is produced. It is nothing to do with the sound of the spray as most cats will sit and observe happily while room air fresheners are being sprayed around.

Getting collared

Contrary to popular belief, a flea collar does not work by preventing fleas from reaching moisture around the cat's eyes or mouth. Fleas have no need of this moisture as they receive plenty from your cat's blood!

Conventional flea collars work by releasing powdered insecticide which spreads gradually over a cat's coat. This spreading action takes time so it will take several days for a new collar to start working efficiently. In the meantime, the cat will continue to attract newly hatched fleas until the insecticide brings them under control. You must ensure that the collar's insecticide is compatible with any environmental spray you may use.

Collars, if used, should be replaced every few months as the insecticide loses its effectiveness with age. The cat's neck should be checked regularly to ensure that no inflammation results. If you have successfully rid the environment of fleas, your cat is being exposed to an unnecessary amount of insecticide if wearing a collar. An RSPCA survey in the 1970s showed that from a sample of

569 cats, 161 were injured or died through wearing flea collars and 408 suffered from dermatitis around the neck.

So think twice about using a flea collar and never use them on young kittens. If you do use a flea collar on your cat, remove it for a few hours each day to allow your cat's skin to breathe. Always remove it if it becomes wet.

With the great interest in herbal alternatives to chemicals, several collar manufacturers are now producing flea collars utilising herbal oils. These do not use chemical insecticides, so will be safer for the cat, but the collars will not kill fleas, only repel them. There will still be fleas in the home but they will probably keep off your cat, and be looking elsewhere (at you?) for their meals. So it is vital that the environment is treated and is completely flea free.

Herbal – and other – flea treatments

Did you know that fleas don't like lemon-flavoured cats? Believers in herbal treatments recommend pouring boiling water over cut-up lemon pieces and leaving the mixture to infuse for several days. The resulting lotion can be rubbed into a cat's coat as a flea repellant.

Feeding a cat garlic is reputed to be a flea repellant as well as discouraging intestinal worms. Homoeopathy provides numerous remedies for the eczema resulting from the irritation caused by flea bites.

Wormwood (*Artemesia absinthium*) is a perennial herb which can be grown in pots or in the garden from seed. It yields a bitter oil which repels fleas. Dried leaves can be rubbed into your cat's coat, then brushed out thoroughly. The leaves can also be placed in a bag in your cat's bed to repel fleas there.

Several manufacturers have taken advantage of the flea-repellant qualities of herbs to produce, not only flea collars, but flea powders, liquids and sprays. There are new applicators too, which are said to produce less stress in a pet. Powder can now be applied when brushing, by an applicator which consists of a brush with holes in the spikes, through which the powder reaches the animal's skin. These products are all advertised in pet magazines from time to time, if your local pet store does not stock them.

There is now a flea repellant in the form of an ultrasonic device which can be placed on a cat's collar or in its bed. The ultrasonic waves are inaudible to humans and said to be inaudible to pets too but their vibrations make it impossible for fleas to attack your pet.

Before all these products were available, cat owners removed fleas from their cats' coats physically by combing them carefully and regularly, using a fine-toothed flea comb. Some owners still feel this is the safest way to remove fleas from their pets but it does take quite an investment in time and has to be done thoroughly and carefully to be effective. If you try this method, have a pan of water handy to drown the fleas in, or throw them in the fire. They're such tough little devils you'll never squash them!

Other 'bugs'

Many flea spray products will also kill lice, mites and ticks.

Lice will suck or bite a cat's skin and can make the cat rundown. There are several types of mite, which burrow into a cat's skin. And ticks will bite and hang on, swelling up with blood, so that they can be confused with a tumour or lump. Don't pull them off as their teeth will still be buried in the cat's skin and an abscess can form. A vet will remove them for you, using chloroform to make them let go. Some owners burn them off using lighted cigarettes which seems a very dangerous undertaking when their cat is probably struggling and complaining about being held down. A drop of clear nail varnish on the tick will make them let go and they can be tweezered off and burnt.

Ringworm is not a bug, nor a worm, but a fungal skin complaint. As its name suggests, it forms a bald patch in a circle of scaly skin on the cat. Veterinary treatment is necessary as it is easily passed from one cat to another, and will consist of antibiotic treatment or an anti-fungal wash for the affected area. Ringworm can be passed from cats to humans but, you will be pleased to hear, we are 'dead-end hosts' and will not pass it on to other people or animals!

Grooming

Brushing and combing

A cat has around 60,000 hairs per square inch on its back, and 120,000 per square inch on its belly. Moggies are not bred for excessive fur length like some pedigrees, so most moggies are perfectly capable of looking after all those hairs themselves.

However, it will benefit any cat to be helped in its grooming by its owner, especially while it is moulting in springtime, or moulting because of stress, when it is old, when it is ill, or just when you think it needs it.

Cat's fur has a 'topcoat' of hairs which are thick, coarse and relatively weatherproof. Their 'undercoat' is soft and downy and provides insulation. In winter, the muscles at the hair roots contract, fluffing out the fur and trapping a layer of air to help keep the cat warm. In summer, the fur thins to help cool the cat.

During this thinning process, it will benefit your cat to be regularly combed or brushed, removing loose hairs it might otherwise swallow. It also prevents your furniture developing a layer of fur!

Steel combs are the most effective grooming aids and are available in several designs. A comb with teeth of equal length is fine for a shorthaired cat but grooming a long-haired cat might be easier using a wide-toothed comb with alternate long and short teeth.

Accustom your cat to grooming from kittenhood and you should not have problems in later life. Start by grooming it without a comb. Simply settle it down on your lap or stand it on a table and gently stroke its fur with your hands, as if you were combing it. When it becomes used to this treatment, comb it regularly for short periods.

Start with the head, back and tail, then the chest. Turn your cat on to its back (easier if you are combing it on your lap) and comb the belly. If your cat refuses to allow this, stand it upright and comb the belly from each side in turn, distracting it from time to time by going back to favourite areas. Every cat has areas it loves being combed: under the chin, behind the ears, or on the tummy. Start and finish your combing on a favourite area and your cat will look forward to its grooming.

You can finish off using a rubber brush, which will collect the rest of the loose hair, especially when the cat is moulting, or a bristle brush which will give shine without causing static.

Even the longest-haired moggies rarely tangle or matt in the way a pedigree longhair will but, if your cat does get some knots in its coat, deal with these as soon as possible or they will only get worse. It will hurt your cat if you try to comb them out so try to unpick them, using your fingers, or cut them out. There is a gadget sold in needlework shops for unpicking stitches and this will unpick coat knots too. Alternatively, insert the blade of a round-ended pair of scissors below the knot and cut upwards. A very-badly knotted coat may have to be dealt with by a vet, who will anaesthetise the cat before cutting off the fur.

Some cats are very up-to-date in their preferred

grooming equipment. A surprising number enjoy being vacuumed while their owners are cleaning the house!

Bathing your cat

Most moggies hate water and detest having baths. Fortunately, bathing a moggy is rarely necessary, unless they fall into some noxious substance which has to be removed.

Cats should be bathed with a proprietary cat shampoo which you can get from a pet store. Don't use human dandruff preparations or washing powder. Equipment should be gathered together before you start and you should trim your cat's claws (see p. 169)! If your cat is used to a harness or a collar you can use this to keep a grip on the cat (don't use a flea collar). If your cat becomes totally unmanageable, you can place it in a sturdy pillowcase and wash it through that.

You will need shampoo, several towels, bowls of warm water and a jug. Place some towelling or a rubber mat in the bottom of the sink for your cat to grip on to and half-fill it with hand-hot water. As cats' coats are fairly waterproof, you may find it difficult to wet it down to the skin, so a few drops of shampoo added to this water will break the surface tension and make it easier to wet your cat thoroughly. Make sure that the room where your cat is to dry off is very warm and draught-free as cats can catch a chill after bathing.

Place your cat in the sink and wet its fur using the water in the sink to which some shampoo has been added, scooping it over the cat with the jug. When it is thoroughly wet, rub in the shampoo, avoiding its head and ears. Rinse thoroughly, using the bowls of warm water, let the water run out, then wrap your cat in a towel and dry it as much as possible. Your cat may shake itself to get rid of the water, so ensure you are still in the kitchen or bathroom. Then wrap another, dry, towel around your cat and rub again. Some cats like to be left wrapped up in another dry towel for warmth as they will feel the cold until they are completely dry. Keep your cat indoors, and warm, for at least the rest of the day.

Sometimes, if your cat is just grubby, it is easier on everyone concerned to give it a dry shampoo. Again, proprietary dry shampoos are available but other substances can be used.

A white cat can be sprinkled with talcum powder, avoiding the face. This is rubbed in, then brushed out, taking any dirt or grease with it. Darker cats can be given a bran bath. Warm the bran in an oven, taking care it doesn't get too hot or it will burn your cat. Rub it into the coat, then brush it out.

Cat litter, in the form of Fullers' earth, makes a good dry shampoo too. Many cats have figured this out for themselves and can often be seen rolling around in their litter trays, or cavorting in patches of dry earth in the garden.

Hairballs

The largest hairball ever removed from a cat was 9 centimetres long, 5 centimetres wide and 3 centimetres thick. Although that is exceptional, hairballs or furballs are formed when small quantities of fur are swallowed as your cat grooms itself. If not expelled, the fur collects in the stomach and forms a hairball.

Indoor cats shed more hair and are more likely to suffer from hairballs than outdoor cats. They can be a problem for longhaired cats and elderly cats too.

A cat with a hairball may vomit without result or be off its food or look miserable. However, these can be symptoms of other problems too, so consult your vet.

Prevention is much better than cure where hairballs are concerned and prevention is not difficult. If you comb or brush your cat regularly, especially when shedding is heaviest, in spring and autumn, hairballs should never be a problem. Stressed cats will also shed more hair and should be groomed more at these times.

You could give your cat an oily fish, such as tinned sardines or mackerel, once a week. This helps ease through any swallowed fur.

There are specific hairball preparations now available which taste attractive to cats and these can be given if you think it is necessary, but not more often than is recommended on the container. Medicinal liquid paraffin is sometimes given to cats with a hairball but this should not be given regularly as it coats the cat's stomach, hastening the passage of food through the stomach and robbing the cat of nourishment.

Claws, eyes, ears and teeth
Lots of cats bite their nails.

This looks odd when an owner first notices it, but what a cat is doing is removing the worn outer casing of the claw. Stropping on a scratching post or tree usually removes this casing, but a cat will sometimes pull it off itself using its teeth. The entire outer casing of the claw can sometimes be found lying on the floor by an owner who thinks the cat has lost a complete claw.

Indoor cats need to have their claws trimmed regularly as they may become overgrown, but most moggies' claws wear down naturally and do not require any attention.

To trim a cat's claws, hold it firmly, then place your finger on the pawpad and your thumb on the top of the paw. Press the pawpad gently and the claws will come forward. Take off just the tip using nail scissors, nail clippers, or trimmers specifically made for trimming claws. Be very careful not to cut off more than the tip. There is a pinkish-coloured quick, which can be seen if you look

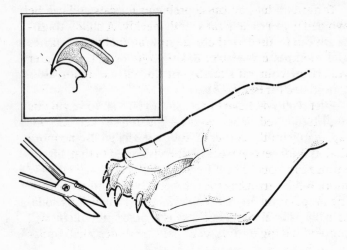

carefully, and claws should never be trimmed to the quick as they will bleed copiously.

Eyes should not need more than an occasional wipe with a dampened piece of cotton wool. Runny eyes may need antibiotic drops from a vet. One owner confused these with his own medicine and used his cat's eyedrops in his ears. He reported he had never been able to hear so well! It just proves that medicines should be treated with great care; it would have done his cat's eyes no good at all to have ear drops used in them.

Moggies' ears rarely need cleaning, unlike some of their big-eared pedigree cousins. If you have to clean your cat's ears, use a cotton bud to gently clean away any excess wax but do not push down into the ear canal.

A cat scratching its ears persistently may have ear mites which should be treated by a preparation from your vet. Inflammation may be present if your cat's ears smell, are reddened inside or have a brown, waxy discharge, so consult your vet.

Tartar buildup can cause problems for cats and can be avoided if you clean a cat's teeth weekly. A child's toothbrush can be used, or there are now animal toothbrushes and toothpaste available. Baking soda or salt and water will clean your cat's teeth, but do not use toothpastes formulated for human use.

First, you will have to accustom your cat to having its mouth touched. When your cat is being stroked on your lap, gently lift the corner of its lip then let go. Do no more than this for several weeks. When it is used to that, lift the lip and run your (clean) finger along its teeth. After a few more weeks, try using the toothbrush without any cleaning preparation on it. Then clean, using the baking soda, salt, or animal toothpaste. This regular treatment will prevent having to have your cat's teeth descaled, under anaesthetic.

It is estimated that 95 per cent of pets over the age of two years suffer from tooth and gum problems. But vets are becoming very sophisticated in dental care – they can offer feline fillings and tooth capping for cats!

Moggy Medicine

You and your vet

Choosing a vet

A friend of mine, when thinking of moving to a new area, first investigates the local vets. If she finds one to her satisfaction, she moves house. After she has moved she finds a doctor for herself.

Choosing a vet, even if you do not go to these lengths, should never be a haphazard operation. Don't ask neighbours who the nearest vet is; don't even ask neighbours who the best vet is. Ask cat-owning neighbours who the best *cat* vet is. Even better, find a knowledgeable local cat breeder and ask her or him. They will soon put you straight!

Some vets are excellent with large animals such as horses. Some are excellent with small animals such as dogs. A good horse vet is not necessarily good with cats and a good dog vet is not necessarily good with cats.

One highly-qualified vet told me that in United Kingdom veterinary schools just twenty years ago, vets were taught nothing about cats. They were taught about dogs – and told to treat cats as small dogs! Remember, those vets are still practising.

In 1984, a working party of the RCVS and BVA in the United Kingdom reported that fewer than 15 per cent of vets were undertaking an acceptable minimum of twenty credit hours of continued training a year, despite continuing advances in diagnostic, surgical and anaesthetic techniques. In the United States, twenty-two states require continued training before veterinary licences are renewed.

So choose carefully and, when you have found a good vet – and there are some very good ones around – build up a relationship through taking your cat for annual booster vaccinations and a check-up, and stock up on any worming or de-fleaing preparations while you are there. Many vets now sell a wide range of other equipment too, such as cat litter and prescription diets, and you should take advantage of their knowledge about all the items they sell or prescribe.

If you have a telephone which is capable of 'memorising' phone numbers, place your vet's number on memory so that, in an emergency, you can quickly contact the surgery.

There are qualified vets who combine homoeopathy, acupuncture, or other 'alternative' treatments with conventional veterinary medicine in the United Kingdom and elsewhere. At least one California vet also uses Bach flower remedies, crystal therapy and colour therapy in her practice. If you feel any of these treatments could benefit your pet, the Royal College of Veterinary Surgeons in London will put you in touch with vets who practise in the United Kingdom.

Many people are shy of addressing their vets because they simply do not know what to call them. All United Kingdom vets have to be Members of the Royal College of Veterinary Surgeons, except for a few remaining elderly vets who are on the supplementary register and became vets before it was necessary to qualify. MRCVS vets are surgeons and, as such, are called Mr, Mrs, Miss or Ms (around half of the students in veterinary schools are now women). Vets with United States or Canadian qualifications are usually Doctors of Veterinary Medicine (DVM) and are referred to as Doctor.

Veterinary medicine has become very sophisticated during this century. Forty or fifty years ago, owners still relied largely on home remedies. Cats which lost their appetites were given a whole kipper to eat, so that the small bones would scour any offending material from their insides. Cuts and bruises were treated with plantain, and a cat with diarrhoea was obliged to swallow crushed clay pipes!

How to give your cat a check-up

Only 47 per cent of United States cat owners take their cats to vets, compared to 74 per cent of dog owners.

Cats don't suffer fewer illnesses than dogs so the difference probably lies with the different make-up of the two animals. A sick dog will jolly well let you know it isn't feeling well but a sick cat may have few symptoms which may not be so apparent if the cat is not around for most of the day. And cats are such stoic creatures that they may not appear off-colour until they are very sick indeed.

So, when giving your cat its weekly grooming session, take the opportunity to give your cat a health check-up too.

Check first for condition of the fur. Is it sleek and glossy or is it dull and patchy? Check for signs of flea infestations; black specks of flea dirt, containing dried blood, which turn red when dampened. Are there any bald spots? Check for scratches or other wounds caused by fights and ensure they are not inflamed. Skin should be clean and neither dry and scaly, nor oily.

Run your hands gently all over your cat's body. Any objection to this may pinpoint a sore spot. Are there any lumps or bumps anywhere? Check the chest area thoroughly. Feel the ribs (if you can't, your cat is too fat!). Gently bend all four limbs (in the direction they are meant to bend) to see if this causes pain.

Run your hands over your cat's head and ensure there are no lumps, bumps, scratches, or sore spots. Look in the ears and check they are clean and do not smell. Eyes should be clear and bright. Check for discharges from the eyes or nose. Look at the teeth and gums; teeth should be clean and breath should not smell excessively (carnivores never have totally sweet breath). Gums should be pink and firm; if they are pale your cat may be anaemic and if they are red, peridontal disease may be the problem. Check that the tongue is clean and shows no sign of ulcers.

Does the skin between the toes look sore and is any foreign object embedded there? Do the claws require trimming?

You can learn to take your cat's pulse and your vet will show you how. Normal heart rate at rest is 100 to 130 beats per minute.

Weigh your cat to ensure weight remains fairly constant. To do this, stand on the bathroom scales and weigh yourself. Then pick up your cat and weigh both of you. Subtract the two figures and you are left with your cat's weight.

You will soon learn what your cat looks like when fit and healthy and may then spot the first tell-tale signs of illness during your regular check-up.

Monitoring your cat's behaviour will also give a clue that your cat may not be feeling well. If it starts to drink more, or urinate more, or have difficulty urinating, eat a lot more or a lot less, loses or gains weight, has any unusual discharges, or diarrhoea or vomiting, shows any change in behaviour (however trivial it may seem), coughs, scratches excessively, does not walk normally, has any open wounds, or you find any lumps, contact your vet immediately.

Don't be afraid to consult your vet if you are worried about your cat; they would rather be consulted over a false alarm than not be consulted when it is necessary. If you are concerned about your cat's health, you need not go to the surgery in the first instance. You can telephone first and explain your worries to the receptionist, who is usually a veterinary nurse. They have undergone veterinary nursing training and will be able to tell you if you should come into the surgery with your cat. They will transfer your telephone call to the vet if you need to discuss anything with him or her.

When you visit the surgery there will be a charge for consultation which will remain the same whatever is wrong with your cat, plus a charge for any medicines prescribed. If surgery has to be carried out, you will be liable for all costs involved. Most vets will make housecalls if your cat is too ill or too nervous to attend the surgery, and there will be an additional charge for this. If veterinary bills are a problem, there are a number of charities which will arrange for veterinary treatment, free of charge, if an owner is unable to pay.

Pet health insurance can be taken out for any pet. It is worth considering as a yearly premium will cover your cat's veterinary bills (excluding the first few pounds of any course of treatment). Usually, the insurance is only available for cats under the age of eight or ten years but a few companies will continue insurance after this age for existing clients. Health insurance companies will not reimburse you for any preventative treatments, such as vaccinations, and usually expenses arising from kittening are not covered. As well as veterinary treatment, health insurance will often provide a lump sum if your cat is killed or lost, and will pay for a reward which you can offer if your cat goes missing.

Information to have ready for your vet

Is your cat eating normally?
If no, is it eating more, less or nothing?

Is your cat drinking normally?
If no, is it drinking more, less or nothing?

Is it producing normal faeces?
If no, does the faeces have an unusual colour, is blood present, or is your cat having difficulty passing its faeces? Does it have diarrhoea?

Has it been vomiting? If so, what? What colour is the vomit?

Has it been coughing? Is there phlegm?

Has it gained or lost weight? Has this been rapid?

Does your cat appear to be in pain? If so, where?

Is your cat walking normally?

Has there been any change in your cat's coat?

Are there any other animals in your household?

Have there been any changes in your household recently?

Have you had any work done in your home recently; e.g. woodworm treatment, redecoration, spring-cleaning?

Has your cat's behaviour changed recently?

Has your cat been in contact with any strange animals; e.g. has it been staying in a cattery?

Major illnesses

Contact your vet immediately if you think your cat may be suffering from any of these illnesses.

Feline Leukaemia Virus

Feline Leukaemia Virus (FeLV) has been described by the more lurid sections of the press as 'the cats' AIDS'. Every time it is described as such, widespread panic ensues among owners terrified of catching AIDS from their cats. In the Soviet Union, the Central Aids Laboratory in Moscow came to a standstill for several days after a false report that cats spread AIDS and cat rescue centres in every country received fifty times as many calls from people wanting to get rid of their cats.

Yet Feline Leukaemia Virus is not transmissible to humans in any form – you *cannot* catch AIDS (or leukaemia) from your cat.

FeLV suppresses a cat's immune system and makes it more vulnerable to other diseases, such as cancer, as well as supressing the bone marrow's production of new blood cells, leading to anaemia.

It is believed that from 30 per cent to 70 per cent of the adult cat population have contracted FeLV at some time, but only about 2 per cent of these become carriers of the disease. FeLV is believed to be transmitted in the saliva, by biting, licking or sneezing.

The incidence of FeLV is slowly decreasing among the pedigree population and slowly increasing among the moggy population due to the different lifestyles of the animals. While many pedigree cats live indoor lifestyles and cannot come into contact with an infected animal, moggies are usually outdoor cats, getting into scraps with other cats which may be infected. All reputable cat breeders insist on FeLV tests before cats are mated, unlike unneutered moggies which make their own arrangements. Although FeLV is not a sexually transmitted disease, as such, a male cat will grip the female's neck in its teeth while mating, often breaking the skin, and disease can be transmitted in this way.

In 1987, FTLV (Feline T-Lymphotropic Lentivirus), a virus in the same group as the AIDS virus, was discovered in a group of cats, and led to further panic among some owners. Professor Oswald Jarrett from the University of Glasgow's Veterinary School believes the virus may have been present in some cats for a very long time but only now that new techniques for finding the AIDS virus have been developed has it been discovered. There is no evidence that this virus is infectious for human beings.

FeLV vaccines are now available in the United States and many European countries but not in the United Kingdom at the time of writing (mid-1988). Vaccinations are given at around nine weeks of age, followed by a second vaccination three weeks later, with a third two months after the second. Annual boosters are then given. The vaccine will protect around 65 per cent of cats but about 10 per cent of cats experienced minor side effects and 0.5 per cent experienced serious side-effects from the vaccines.

At the time of writing there is no cure for FeLV or FTLV and cats with the virus should be isolated from other cats. Euthanasia may have to be considered as an option for a positive testing cat.

Symptoms include lack of appetite and weight loss, fever, general malaise, swollen glands, and blood in faeces.

This is a disease about which there is still a great deal of fear and ignorance among the general public. One cat owner, after having the facts about FeLV explained to her at great length, said firmly: 'Well, I don't have to worry about my cats catching it. None of them is gay!'

Feline Enteritis (Panleucopaenia)

The mortality rate of cats contracting this disease (also called feline distemper) is high – up to 100 per cent at times. Yet it is a preventable disease with yearly vaccination available, which is given combined with vaccine for upper respiratory infections.

The virus is shed in urine, faeces, saliva and vomit and can persist in the environment for up to a year. It attacks body cells, especially the lining of the bowel, reducing the numbers of white cells in the blood.

Symptoms include a high temperature, sunken eyes, withdrawal and a painful abdomen as the infection inflames the bowel. The cat may hang over its water bowl as if it would like to drink, but is unable to, and dehydration often occurs. There will be vomiting, usually of a bile-stained (greenish) liquid and the cat will seek seclusion. However, some cats show few symptoms and young kittens may die before showing any symptoms at all.

Treatment consists of antibiotics and fluids given intravenously. Blood transfusions may be given. Nursing care is very important. With this disease, as with others, if an owner is willing to spend time nursing their cats, their Tender Loving Care can make an enormous difference to the outcome.

Feline Infectious Peritonitis

FIP is most common in cats under three years of age and about 20 per cent of the cats exposed to this viral disease will contract it. Cats whose immune system has been depressed by FeLV are more likely to contract the disease.

There are two forms: wet FIP with fluid accumulation in the abdominal cavity, giving the cat a swollen appearance, and dry FIP with enlargement of various organs. In the dry form, symptoms depend on which organ is affected but can include loss of appetite, fever, withdrawal and anaemia.

There is no vaccine against FIP and no cure, and euthanasia must be considered for affected cats. A 'replacement' cat or kitten should not be brought into the household for at least a month.

Feline Respiratory Disease

Often incorrectly referred to as cat 'flu, FRD is a common infection caused by a number of viruses. The most commonly involved are rhinotracheitis and calicivirus.

Both viruses cause sneezing, fever and discharges from the nose and eyes which can become encrusted, and mouth ulcers. The disease is spread by affected cats sneezing infected droplets over other cats, which is why boarding catteries should always have 'sneeze barriers' between pens and why they should insist on seeing your cat's certificate of vaccination before allowing it to stay.

An affected cat will often refuse to eat because of mouth ulcers and because its sense of smell has been impaired (a cat's appetite is stimulated by scent). An owner prepared to give an affected cat lots of TLC will have an important effect on the outcome as, otherwise, many cats seem to give up their will to live. Fluids and liquid, strong-smelling foods will have to be given by the owner, who will often have to persuade the cat to take them. Eye and nose discharges will have to be wiped and ointment be applied. Antibiotics and eye drops will often be prescribed.

This often fatal disease can be almost completely prevented by yearly vaccinations (see 'Moggy Maintenance', p. 155).

Feline Urological Syndrome

The formation of struvite crystals can irritate the bladder

wall, causing cystitis and can cause a complete blockage, especially in male cats. When complete blockage occurs, the affected cat can die, if treatment is not carried out swiftly. With some urological problems, effects are relatively mild, and it may not be apparent that the cat is suffering from them.

Symptoms are blood in the urine, straining in the litter box (sometimes mistaken for constipation), excessive licking of the vulva or penis, and a twitching tail. The cat may refuse to use its litter box, soil outside the box, or show pain when urinating.

The full cause is not known but it is thought that many factors contribute to the incidence of FUS. These can include a virus, stress, alkaline urine, too-early neutering of male cats, and diet, including excessive magnesium in the diet. At one time, dry foods were implicated in the formation of struvite crystals because they were dry, decreasing the amount of urine formed, and because they were high in magnesium. Now prescription diets are available which, although dry, are specially formulated to help cats with a tendency to urological problems. These are available from your vet.

Predisposing factors to FUS include a sedentary lifestyle (a cat will urinate less often if lazy) and restricted access to the outside world. Urine volume should be kept high so cats should be encouraged to drink plenty of water (perhaps by adding a little salt to its meals) and the urine kept acidic – a vet may prescribe a urinary acidifier. Urine remains more consistently acidic if several small meals are fed each day rather than one large one. If giving dry food (other than a prescription diet for FUS) soak it in water, stock or broth before feeding.

In serious cases, a vet will have to clear the obstruction by inserting a thin tube into the bladder.

Feline Dysautonomia (Key Gaskell Syndrome)

This disease was first recognised in 1981, and named after T. J. A. Key and Professor C. J. Gaskell who were first to describe it in 1982. Recovery from the disease can be as low as 10 per cent to 30 per cent.

It interferes with the part of the cat's nervous system which stimulates heart, lungs and other internal organs, and glands.

Cats suffering from the disease may avoid bright light, as their pupils are dilated, saliva dries up and the cat may lose its appetite as any food eaten will be regurgitated. Constipation will also be a problem.

There is, at the moment, no cure for the disease but the symptoms can be alleviated with eye drops, a fluid diet and treatment for constipation.

Rabies

Only the United Kingdom, Australia, New Zealand, Hawaii and Scandinavia (apart from Finland) are free from rabies.

Infection is spread when a rabid animal bites another, and rabies can be passed on to humans, if bitten. In a cat, symptoms include apprehension, a change of personality, and dislike of lights and noise. By the time a cat shows any symptoms, it is already infectious, and death is inevitable.

If a cat has been exposed to rabies, immediate treatment, using antiserum and vaccination, may be successful. Vaccinations against rabies are available and should be given at the age of three months, with yearly boosters.

A human bitten by a rabid animal should wash out the wound thoroughly, apply antiseptic, and seek immediate medical attention.

First Aid

Be extremely wary if trying to assist an injured cat which is not your own – and careful if it is your own cat. Pain and shock can make the best-natured cat bite and scratch. If a cat has been injured but is conscious, wear thick gloves if you can, to protect yourself. A struggling cat can be transported by wrapping it in a thick jacket, taking care not to exacerbate any injuries.

First Aid is, of course, just that – the first things you can do to help a cat until you are able to transport it to a vet. Never give pain-killers as many are toxic to cats, and do not attempt home remedy antidotes to poison or burns. Never give a cat alcohol.

Breathing difficulties

If a cat has stopped breathing, check that the mouth and throat are unobstructed. Place the animal on its side, if possible, and extend the head, pulling the tongue forward. Place your hand on the ribs with your other hand on top of that. Press down gently and release immediately; repeat fifteen times per minute.

If the cat has been in water and is unconscious, hold it upside down by the hind legs for about twenty seconds and shake several times to clear the airways of water.

Artificial respiration can be applied; hold its mouth and lips closed and blow into its nostrils. Blow until the chest rises then let the animal exhale six to ten times per minute. If it does not, press the chest to expel the air.

Cardiac arrest

Check for heartbeat by placing your fingertips on the lower part of the chest, behind the front leg, or by listening to the left side of the animal's chest.

If the heart has stopped, place the cat on its side and

place your hand on the middle of its chest. Press down firmly but gently (you could crush its ribs if you apply too much pressure) for a count of two and release for a count of one. Repeat sixty times per minute, using artificial respiration (above) at the same time.

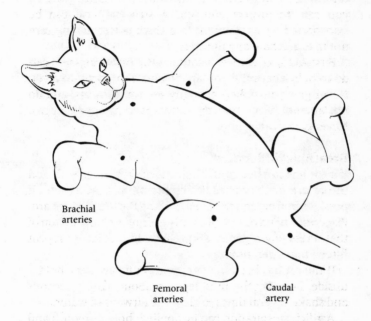

Brachial
arteries

Femoral
arteries

Caudal
artery

External bleeding

Press on the bleeding area using a clean cloth or bandage. If this does not stop the flow, compress the pressure points (see above). In severe cases of injury to a leg or tail, a tourniquet can be applied but must be loosened every five minutes to allow oxygen to the tissues, before being reapplied.

Loop a bandage or scarf twice around the injured tail or leg above the wound and tie a half knot. Place a short stick on top of the half knot and complete the knot. Twist the stick until bleeding stops. Remember to loosen it every five minutes if it takes longer than this to seek veterinary attention.

Burns
Immerse the cat up to the neck in cold water for at least five minutes, then transport it to a vet. Telephone the vet while the cat is being immersed, if you can, to alert him or her of your imminent arrival. Do not remove any loose skin or blisters, and do not apply *any* ointments, salves or any other home remedy – they will have to be scraped off again before the cat can be treated.

Heat prostration
Your cat may be suffering from heat prostration if it is breathing very rapidly, staggering, or its tongue, which will appear bright red, is hanging out. If these symptoms are severe, treat in a similar manner to burns. Immerse in cold water up to the neck, then transport the cat to a vet. Less severe cases may respond if the cat is placed in a cool area.

Shock
A shocked cat will have a low temperature, appear confused and weak, have cold feet and may be shivering, and the skin will appear pale.

Place the cat on its side with head extended in a comfortable place, if possible. Check the mouth and throat are clear and pull forward the tongue if the cat is unconscious. Speak soothingly to the cat and keep it warm by wrapping it in a jacket. Transport the cat to a vet as soon as possible.

Poisoning
Symptoms of poisoning include vomiting, diarrhoea, fits and a staggering gait. A poisoned cat should be left in a

secure, dark place while you immediately telephone your vet. If you know what has caused the poisoning, inform your vet over the telephone so that antidotes can be prepared without delay. Scrutinise containers so that the poisonous substance can be identified.

Kittening

As it is really performing no service to catkind by leaving a female cat unspayed, you may only have to refer to this section if you take in a pregnant 'stray'. She won't be a stray, of course, but a pet which was not spayed and was thrown out when she became pregnant.

Moggies will become fertile early in the first spring after they have passed the age of six months or so. As cats remain pregnant for around 63–65 days, this means that the kittens will be born in the warmth of summertime, and enables them to grow and thrive in the months before the onset of winter.

Female cats on heat (in oestrus) will roll and call dramatically, raising their rear ends into a receptive position. Owners seeing this for the first time often think the cat has been injured and is in pain, but this is not the case.

If you have delayed having your cat spayed and she comes into heat, she cannot be spayed until the heat has finished, some five to seven days later, as she is more likely to haemorrhage during this time. During the oestrus period, she must be kept indoors away from all un-neutered tomcats. This is easier said than done, as a cat in heat is extremely crafty and has only one thought in mind – to get out and mate. You will have to put up with a lot of noisy caterwauling during this time, and the presence outside of dozens of tomcats, drawn from far and wide by the female's scent – but it is your own fault; you should have had her spayed!

A pregnant cat will show the first signs after about three weeks when she pinks up – her nipples become larger and redder. She will gain weight and will have an increased appetite. During pregnancy, a female should be fed top-quality food – and as much as she wants of it. A good vitamin supplement should be added to her food.

Moggies usually – but not always – have no difficulty in giving birth, but this doesn't mean they should be left to get on with it by themselves. The presence of a caring owner is always appreciated, and is essential if it is the cat's first litter.

The first sign that birth is imminent may be the female looking for a nesting site. Prepare one for her and place it in a quiet position which is convenient for you and which she will accept. A good kittening box can be made by cutting down a large cardboard carton. Use one which has had 'clean' contents such as packets of crisps and not one which has contained boxes of soap powder which will smell of detergent. Place another, larger box over the first, with a hole cut in the side which is large enough for your hands to go through, to assist at the birth.

The cat will be much happier with the box if it is in a quiet position, is fairly dark and secluded inside, and if it is not moved, unless she showed she did not like the first position in which you placed it. Cover the bottom with many sheets of newspaper, for warmth, and cover the newspaper with clean kitchen paper, which can be removed and replaced regularly once the box is in use.

When the first contractions start, the female will probably go to her kittening bed, although she may wake you up to tell you about it first. Kittens, like most mammals, are usually born at night, and often around the full moon. She may pant a little or purr and there may be a clear discharge, or a spot of blood. This stage can last as long as six to twelve hours but is usually much less than that.

Contractions will then start, lasting ten to thirty minutes (if they last longer than ninety minutes without producing a kitten, telephone your vet) and the first kitten will be expelled. The cat may then open the birth sac in which it is contained, and shear the umbilical cord with her teeth. However, in many cases, this is left to the owner! Gently (but quickly) grasp the skin of the sac, pull it away from the kitten inside and tear. It tears extremely easily and scissors should not be used for this.

Leave the umbilical cord intact for the moment, while you ensure the kitten's nose is clear and it can breathe. Then, if all is well, rub the fur dry gently with a rough, but clean, towel. Then tie some cotton thread a couple of inches from the kitten's navel. Cut the cord on the placenta side, using scissors which have been sterilised. Immediately place the kitten at its mother's belly, so that it can find a teat and she can lick it and assure herself all is well.

While you have been assisting, your cat may have

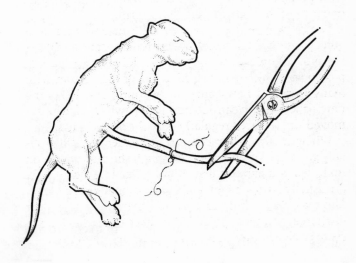

produced another kitten and you can start the process again if the mother shows no inclination to break the sacs. Sometimes, a cat will deal with one or two kittens itself, but leave the others, and this is where the owner should help. The cat may start to eat the placentas and it is believed they have some function in starting the milk to flow. Allow her to eat at least one if she shows any inclination to do so but more than that may cause a tummy upset.

Ensure that your cat is kittening in a warm room and that the kittens, once born, are quickly returned to the mother for her body heat and helped to find a teat. A heating pad or heat lamp may be useful. New-born kittens can lose heat very rapidly and, if you find one is cold and sluggish, you should immerse it up to the neck in hand-warm water.

If any one of the kittens is having difficulty breathing, hold it at arm's length in the palms of your hand, and swing your arms downward, stopping abruptly with the kitten's nose pointing towards the floor. Repeat this several times until breathing is restored and the kitten begins to cry and wriggle.

Call the vet if at any time your cat seems uneasy or distressed, if she strains for more than an hour without success, if there is more than three hours between kittens, or if she passes a yellow or green discharge, or blood, before the kittens are born.

After the birth is over, leave the mother and kittens in peace with a water bowl, food and a litter tray nearby. New mothers may not eat or drink for a day or two, or use their tray, so try to encourage them to do so. They will certainly not want to be out of sight of the kittens at first.

Even if all goes well, it is a good idea to have a vet check over the cat and kittens the day after birth to ensure that all are well and that all kittens in the uterus have been expelled. If, for any reason, your cat is unable to feed the kittens, you will be able to purchase a milk replacement substitute from your vet or pet store, and will have to feed the kittens at two-hourly intervals, using a dropper or special animal feeding bottle. The kittens' tummies should be gently rubbed and their bottoms cleaned soon after feeding to help them eliminate waste matter; they are unable to do this by themselves for about four weeks.

Keep visitors strictly away for the first few weeks and only let visitors handle older kittens if they have thoroughly washed their hands first. Infections can be passed on very easily to young kittens.

The likelihood is that all will go well and the new kittens will fascinate you so much that you will hardly be able to tear yourself away from them and their antics for the next two months until they are ready to leave their mother!

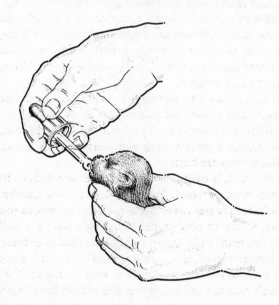

Problem Pages

Who's got a problem?

All of us!
I used to think that about 95 per cent of cat owners had problems with their cats at one time or another. Now I believe the figure is much higher!

So if you have turned to these pages because you need help with a problem, don't take it personally. Many owners seem to think that they have failed in some way if a cat soils where it shouldn't or tears the furniture.

As long as you understand the reason for your cat's behaviour, you can do something about it.

The cat is the number one pet numerically in the United Kingdom, the United States and in a number of European countries. This is not just due to its charm as a pet, but to today's lifestyle.

Many people have busier lives than ever before, yet they still crave the company of pets. With good reason; for interacting with a pet has been proved to lower heart rate and blood pressure, pet owners live longer than non pet-owners, and children brought up with pets learn about responsibility to others.

But with today's lifestyle, what is the best sort of pet to buy? Dogs have lost their number one position because busy people haven't time to take them for walks, and disposing of their waste products has become a matter of public concern. Fish and birds do not fulfil human needs for touch and other small mammals are usually kept in cages.

So, often the cat is seen as the ideal, 'easy' pet to keep.

They don't need to be taken for walks, there is no cage to clean out, and they usually make their own toilet arrangements – but, despite all this, they are *not* 'easy' pets.

They are complex creatures, guided by instinct, and need our knowledge and understanding to enable them to live happily with us.

Of course, our ideas of what constitutes a problem differ. One owner will live with a spraying cat or shredded furniture and barely notice, while another will consider these problems grounds for rehoming the cat, if they continue.

Buy your home to suit your cat

That isn't entirely a flippant suggestion. Dedicated cat owners do consider their cats' needs when moving house.

If you are happy living in your present home, I'm not suggesting that you should move to suit your cat; but, if you are thinking of moving, consider not only if it is suitable for you but if it is suitable for your cat too.

I recently decided not to buy a new house because it was not sunny enough for one of my cats which stays indoors all the time and enjoys its safe sunbathing through the windows. Many other people I know have turned down otherwise perfect homes because they were unsuitable in some way for their cats – and had their estate agents tearing their hair out.

But your cat is a member of your family too and deserves consideration. Cat rescue organisations recognise this and will often refuse to rehome a cat if the home is considered unsuitable because of size or location.

Many problems can be avoided if you decorate and furnish your home to suit your cat. If wallpapering, don't choose a hessian-type paper if you don't want your cat to climb the walls. Some cats insist on climbing curtains; it's easier to choose blinds instead, if you don't want to spend time discouraging your cat from this activity.

Smooth fabrics are better on furniture than textured fabrics, which tempt cats to strop on them. I've found that Irish linen loose covers stand up best to numerous pairs of catty claws. If you bought your settee before you bought your cat and it is being damaged, cover the scratched parts with plastic sheeting; cats hate to feel this under their paws and will leave it alone while you encourage them to use their scratching post instead. And loop pile carpets are a disaster with cats in the house; the loops are 'pulled' by even the best-behaved cat's claws. If your cat's fur is dark, dark-coloured carpets won't show up so much moulted fur in the springtime. Light-coloured fur won't show up so much on light-coloured carpets.

If you're worried about your ornaments, a little modelling clay or Blu-Tack will fix them to your shelves, so that they can't be knocked over by inquisitive cats.

Cats will often eat houseplants because they need green matter as an aid to digestion. You can buy cocksfoot grass seeds from many pet suppliers and grow a little tub for your cat to chew instead. My cats continue to eat the houseplants anyway, so now I provide them with their own houseplants which they are allowed to eat; umbrella plants are favourites. Precious plants can be protected by dabbing their leaves with diluted Tabasco sauce or sprinkling them with pepper.

If your cat digs up the soil from your potted plants, provide it with a litter tray if it doesn't already have one. Prevent it from more gardening by covering the soil with a wire mesh circle, or surround the plant with cooking foil.

Care should be taken in the selection of house and garden plants as many are toxic to cats (see 'Cats in Danger', p. 145).

House-training

House-training doesn't mean quite the same thing for cats as for dogs. Only very rarely does a young kitten need training in using its litter tray; the behaviour happens naturally almost as soon as they are able to walk to it.

However, if you do acquire a kitten which has not been provided with a tray, and consequently hasn't learned to use one, it should be very easy to train because it will be keen to learn. Cats are extremely fastidious creatures and being unable to dispose of their waste products in a natural manner distresses them terribly.

Between half an hour to an hour after your kitten has been fed, place it on its litter tray (which should be kept in one spot to prevent confusion). Then use your fingers to scratch up the litter for a few moments. The kitten will look interested and may begin to scratch too. This will often lead to instinct taking over and the kitten will relieve itself. If it isn't ready to do so, place it back on the tray half an hour later or when you see it squatting down in an inappropriate place.

The training your cat or kitten will need is in the rules of your home. Remember that you are chief cat (see 'Cat Conduct', p. 64) and that your cat expects to be disciplined by you as it would be disciplined by a more dominant cat if living in a feral group.

Discipline does not mean shouting at your cat and never means smacking it as cats will lose all confidence in owners who resort to these measures.

But, if your cat is misbehaving, for example, stropping on the furniture instead of its scratching post, do remonstrate with it. Take it away from whatever it is doing, speaking to it at the same time in a firm voice. Glaring at it works very well too! Cats are very clever and soon understand the word 'no' if spoken firmly and sharply.

(Remember to praise it when it does use its scratching post.)

You must remember to say no *every* time your cat misbehaves. Sometimes they will deliberately misbehave while watching you for your reaction. If there is no reaction, they decide it is all right to carry on with whatever they are doing, and the habit will become hard to break. So be firm and be consistent.

A cat will often do something it knows it is not allowed to do and might even ignore your reprimand. In which case, a soft, well-aimed cushion works wonders!

With a recalcitrant cat, aversion therapy can be used as a last resort. Keep a filled water pistol handy and, when the cat misbehaves, give it a quick squirt. Cats hate getting wet and will soon link the misbehaviour with a soaking and will learn not to do it. A water pistol (or clean washing-up liquid container) is useful for training because the cat will not associate the process of getting wet with you. If it did, it might become nervous of you.

Soiling in the home

If your cat wets the carpet, it's a cry for help.

Some owners think their cats urinate or defaecate on floors or furniture in order to 'spite' them. But cats will only behave like this if there is something wrong with them. It is the only way they have of alerting their owners to a problem.

Indiscriminate soiling is often the first sign of an illness. Quite a few cats will suffer from a urinary condition at some time in their lives and this may be the first symptom an owner sees. It is vital that immediate veterinary attention is sought. Delay could cost the life of your cat while suitable treatment will often bring a swift cure.

Stress can result in soiling. Sometimes an owner will

scold a cat for misbehaviour and the cat will then soil indoors. This is not to get its own back – the scolding has caused the cat to feel stressed.

There are many other causes of stress to cats. Any change in the household, with a family member leaving or joining, a house move, a divorce, a new baby, another pet, even new furniture can trigger this behaviour. Patience and understanding are the only answers to soiling caused by stress. Don't smack your cat; it isn't doing anything wrong and it won't understand, and you'll simply add to its stress level and the likelihood of the behaviour continuing.

If you don't provide your cat with a litter tray, it may soil because it can't get outside quickly enough, or because there is something unpleasant out of doors; another cat or deep snow!

If your cat has a litter tray but uses the carpet instead, this may be due to confusion. Cats 'cover up' with litter but sometimes they have their paws outside the tray while doing this. If they feel carpet under their paws, they become confused, thinking this is their litter medium. If this is your cat's problem, set the litter tray on a large piece of plastic sheeting, or provide a covered tray which will prevent your cat's paws from scratching outside.

The litter you choose might lead to soiling outside the tray. Cats have their own preferences and may refuse to use a type they do not like, especially if they contain additives, such as deodorants. Trays should always be kept clean and, if possible, cleaned out as soon as they are used (after all, who wants to use a dirty toilet?).

As urine and faeces are used to mark territory, a cat may not use a tray another cat has used, even if it has since been cleaned. If you have more than one cat, try to have more than one tray.

Clean the trays with a solution of diluted sodium

hypochlorite (household bleach). Some disinfectants are toxic to cats and they won't use a tray which has been washed with them.

Old age and tummy upsets can lead to soiling too. You can only be patient and provide extra trays.

Spraying in the home

Contrary to belief, both males and females spray. It is, of course, only a problem when the spraying takes place indoors.

Some owners confuse spraying with urination. When a cat urinates, it will squat down to do so. To spray, a cat will stand upright, back up to a vertical object such as a wall or door, raise its tail high and spray a backwards jet of urine.

Neutered cats are less likely to spray than unneutered cats, as well as being more pleasant to have around!

Occasionally, spraying behaviour will occur in a neutered cat because the operation has been incompletely carried out and some testicular tissue remains. This will continue to produce the male hormone, testosterone and the cat will continue to behave like an unneutered tomcat. A veterinary visit will be necessary to monitor the levels of testosterone and if any tissue remains, this can be removed surgically or hormone levels can be adjusted by a course of drugs.

Spraying can occur if an owner has more than one cat. The cat then begins to mark its territory inside the home by spraying. It could help if you give the cat some space of its own in the house – a room in which to sleep away from the other cats, for example. The danger number of cats seems to be four – often the addition of a fourth cat leads to spraying (or soiling) problems. In severe cases, careful rehoming with a sympathetic owner can stop the behaviour.

Stress can also result in spraying – the stress of any

change in routine, illness, or the presence nearby of a strange cat.

A male cat may also spray in response to a female in season, even if she is some distance away. Although this is more likely in an unneutered cat, neutered cats will sometimes respond in this way.

If you have a cat which sprays so much that you can no longer share your home with it, but you don't want to rehome it, you could consider making or buying a cat chalet with a run in which it can live in the garden. It will of course need heating and lighting and your company as often as possible.

Sprayed or soiled areas must be thoroughly cleaned so that the cat is not triggered by the smell to use the area again. Wash with clean water, then a solution of water and sodium hypochlorite (remember it is a bleach so test a small area first for colour fastness). To completely eradicate smells, sprinkle the area with dry baking soda. This will absorb the water and can be vacuumed up when it dries out.

Deter your cat from using the area again with a proprietary deterrent from a pet store, or try vinegar, oil of peppermint, citrus oils or pepper. Plastic sheeting or cooking foil placed over the area will often discourage further use.

If your problem is a strange cat which sprays around your doors or in your garden, cover its favourite spraying areas with cooking foil. It will hate the noise of the liquid hitting the foil and will move on elsewhere!

Biting the hand . . .

If your cat bites you when you tickle its tummy, stop tickling its tummy!

The fighting posture of the cat is duplicated when you do this as cats will try to fight from a position underneath, when their opponent will scrabble away with its back legs on their stomach. A cat can become temporarily confused and bite its owner.

Other cats simply become over-stimulated when being stroked. They enjoy it at first but watch out for a thrashing tail. This means they have had enough and you should stop.

A cat will often grasp its owner's hand or wrist to stop them doing something the cat would rather they didn't do. This is not a true bite, more a restraint, but it looks the same to an owner!

Sometimes a cat will ambush an owner, jumping out and biting as the owner passes. The cat is really trying to play but in an inappropriately rough way. Carry a few small toys around with you and, if your cat jumps out, quickly drop a toy. Its playfulness should redirect itself towards the toy instead of your shins.

A cat which suddenly starts to bite may do so because it is feeling ill, so a veterinary consultation is necessary if this behaviour begins for no apparent reason.

Squabbles among cats are not uncommon but should be minimised if introductions have been carried out carefully (see 'Introductions', p. 45).

Minimise confrontations as much as possible between squabbling cats. Give them separate feeding bowls well spaced apart and separate sleeping areas if necessary.

If one cat is neutered and another is entire, fights will almost certainly result, so ensure cats are neutered at the age recommended by your vet.

Again, if one of the cats is feeling ill, fights may break out. And if one cat has been away from home for a few days, for example at the vet's, scrapping may start. This is because the cat which has been away will now smell strange to the other cat. They usually settle down again in a couple of days.

A hormone imbalance might be the cause of friction and can be remedied by a course of treatment from your vet.

There are also herbal nerve tonic tablets specifically for pets, available from pet shops, which might help the situation if your cat is feeling run down and unhappy.

If you can find no other cause for aggressive behaviour in your cat, you might consider its environment. Cats will sometimes react in an aggressive manner due to toxins in their environment. If your home has recently been painted or treated with chemicals, consider that this might be the cause of the behaviour.

Some cats react badly to the ingredients in their food, even if they have been eating the same food for some time without ill effects. Try changing its food to another brand, if you feed it a proprietary food. It seems that some cats have an allergic reaction to some foods, or additives in the food, in the same way some humans react aggressively to additives in processed food.

Boredom

It surprises many people to learn that cats can become bored. But they are intelligent and active animals and need mental and physical stimulation in the same way we do.

If they are left indoors day after day while an owner goes out to work they can become very bored and will try to find something to entertain themselves. If no toys are provided, the entertainment may take the form of stripping wallpaper off the wall or knocking down the ornaments. This is not naughtiness; this is just something to *do*.

Ideally, cats should have companions. If their human companion cannot be with them for large portions of the day, provide a feline companion who can.

The Pensioner Puss

Looking after the older cat

You'll never see a cat with false teeth. Dogs are some-times fitted with false teeth, but never cats, because (as long as they are kept from aggressive cats and don't have to use them to protect themselves) they don't need teeth. They can adapt to life very well without them, just as most cats adapt well to their old age.

At what age does a cat become old? Opinions vary and cats themselves age at radically different rates. One cat may be old at 10 years while another shows few signs of aging at 18 or 20 years. There are Peter Pans in the cat world too!

Some authorities consider a cat old at 9 years while others say a cat is not old until the age of 14 years, at which time they equate to a 70-year-old human. A 20-year-old cat equates with a 100-year-old human and should be receiving its telegram from the Queen or the White House! The world's oldest cat whose age could be authenticated was a female tabby moggy called Ma, who died in Devon in 1957, aged 34 years 5 months. Like humans, cats will live longer if they have picked the right parents; long-lived parents tend to have long-lived offspring.

Be aware of the signs of aging in your cat and try to make its golden years as comfortable as you can. It will certainly slow down, becoming much less active than before as its body undergoes many changes. It may be-come less concerned about its surroundings and more interested in, and dependent on, its owner. If your cat was always short-tempered, it may mellow. It may sleep for longer periods, eat smaller amounts more often, drink more, become less tolerant of noise and children, become restless and sometimes be unable to get to its litter tray in time.

It is important to continue an elderly cat's vaccinations. Although some cats have built up an incredible resistance to illness by old age, others will have a lowered tolerance. Older cats usually dislike change and new surroundings, so a yearly veterinary check-up and vaccinations can be less stressful if you ask your vet to make a housecall, instead of taking your cat to the surgery. There will be an additional charge for a housecall but your older cat will be happier with the arrangement and, if you have several cats and have them all checked at the same time, the reduction in stress to *you* in catching them all and trans-porting them to the surgery could make a housecall well worth while.

Your vet will want to check your cat's teeth, among other things. Tartar will build up on a cat's teeth through the years and, if neglected, will lead to gum disease and your cat will be reluctant to eat as it will be painful to do so. The professional cleaning of a cat's teeth will involve using an anaesthetic, which always carries a slight risk, but particularly so for an older cat. Once your vet has removed any tartar buildup, you can clean your cat's teeth at home to prevent a recurrence.

If you have cleaned your cat's teeth since it was young (see 'Moggy Maintenance', p. 17) it will make its old age more comfortable. If you have not cleaned your cat's teeth, it may not be too late to start as long as you are patient. If your cat begins to drool, this could be a symptom of decay or tartar on the teeth and veterinary advice should be sought as soon as possible.

Feeding the pensioner puss

Why is Spaghetti Bolognese an ideal addition to an older cat's diet?

An older cat has quite different dietary requirements to that of a younger cat. Older cats should be fed less protein than young cats, but it should be higher quality protein (see 'Nutrition for Cats', p. 108). Carbohydrates should be increased, so add pasta, rice, potato or bread to your cat's food. A remarkable number of cats enjoy Spaghetti Bolognese and this can be added to your cat's diet along with other pastas and rice cooked in meaty stocks to tempt your cat's appetite.

Too much protein makes your cat's kidneys work too hard and kidney disease is regularly found among older cats. Your vet will advise on diet which may include white meats and fish and exclude red meats. Prescription diets for older cats are also available from vets, and these are specially formulated for an older cat's needs.

An older cat needs less protein, more fat and carbohydrates, less magnesium, phosphorus and calcium and increased vitamins. Authorities differ as to what these increased vitamins should be, but some believe that supplementation of vitamins B_{12}, C and E may be beneficial.

Constipation may become a problem with the less-active cat. Veterinary advice should be sought and a vet will often recommend the addition of a little bran to food, or feeding food to which water, stock or soup has been added to make a thick broth.

Your cat may become fatter with advancing years. This should not be encouraged as slim cats have longer life expectancies than fat cats. Provide smaller meals (which can be fed more often) and provide no snacks between meals. Your cat may be demanding food as a way of getting more attention. If you suspect this is the cause, a daily gentle play session (see 'Indoor or outdoor cat?', p. 91) could be extremely beneficial.

Eating may be difficult for an older cat if it is expected to eat from a low bowl. Joint stiffness may make it painful for the cat to bend as far as required. It will benefit if its food and water bowls are raised slightly, by placing them on a low stool or platform. If your cat cannot reach its favourite sleeping place, a stool placed beneath it will be appreciated.

Care for the older cat

Walking upstairs may not be as easy for your cat as it once was, so there should be litter trays (which should always be provided for elderly cats) upstairs and downstairs. Even so, your cat may occasionally have an 'accident' and you should deal with this patiently, without scolding. An older cat will not have so much control over its muscles as it once had and scolding it will only make it nervous and increase its stress levels.

Older cats, with stiffening joints, may not be able to groom themselves very well. Even if you have left your cat to groom itself throughout its life, start to comb it regularly now. There are many parts of its body it will no longer be able to reach and regular combing will make the cat feel better, as well as reducing the risk of furballs forming which your cat's aging muscles may be unable to expel. Older cats sometimes develop skin complaints and veterinary attention should be sought as soon as this is noticed.

Sometimes the dewclaw (the claw part way up the back of the leg) will overgrow, forming a circle which can penetrate the flesh. Check your cat's dewclaws at least once a month, for overgrown dewclaws can become infected. An overgrown dewclaw can be trimmed by an owner but seek veterinary advice if you are unsure which end to cut – it can sometimes be difficult to tell which end is which.

Some cats may go partially deaf or their eyesight may deteriorate; these cats should be encouraged to spend their remaining days indoors. Even cats which have been very active out of doors when younger, may welcome the opportunity to stay indoors in later life. Cats should not be allowed out at night as a general rule and older cats should not be expected to spend nights out of doors or to use an outside toilet at night. Old animals also need additional heat so, if your cat does not have a warm place to rest or sleep, provide it with a pet-heating pad (do not use an electric blanket for humans).

Older cats will desire some peace and privacy so, if you have visitors to stay, make sure there is a quiet place to which your cat can escape.

Try not to change your cat's routine, if possible. When going on holiday, an older cat will be less upset by a neighbour coming in to feed it than it would by having to spend time in a cattery. If a cat has never stayed in a cattery, it should not be expected to once it reaches the age of eight or ten. A cat which spends some time each year in the same cattery and is used to the surroundings and the staff, may still be able to spend time there without ill effect even at quite an advanced age.

Although it may seem that older cats are more 'work', many owners find that they need to make few adjustments to suit their cats' advancing years, and these are made gradually and almost unnoticeably. And who would begrudge an old friend a few extra comforts?

Illnesses of the older cat

One illness you are unlikely to see in the older cat is that scourge of mankind, heart disease. No one knows quite why, but even dogs are ten times more likely to suffer from heart conditions than cats.

Veterinary check-ups for elderly cats are essential at least once a year but contact your vet immediately if your cat loses weight, starts eating more food and drinking more water, eats less food and drinks less water, or if there is any marked change in its normal behaviour.

Kidney failure can be common in the older cat with as many as three-quarters of cats over the age of ten years experiencing it. The earliest symptom is an increased consumption of water. Kidney disease can be controlled by feeding the correct diet but, as with most illnesses, the earlier treatment begins, the better the chances of success.

Hyperthyroidism is now the most common illness of older cats. It is caused by the thyroid gland producing too much hormone, which speeds up the metabolism and can lead to heart failure. Symptoms are increased appetite and water consumption, with some cats becoming hyperactive or even aggressive. It can be treated by drugs, radiotherapy or surgery, if recognised in time.

Diabetes Mellitus can develop in the older cat and symptoms include increased appetite and water consumption, coupled with loss of weight. Most cats respond well to daily insulin injections which the owner learns to give and the cat can enjoy life for many years to come.

Cats can also suffer from cancer and the incidence appears to increase between the ages of ten to fifteen, decreasing after the age of 15. According to the Animal Health Trust, the incidence of tumours is higher in cats and dogs than in humans. All types of treatment used in human therapy are applicable to cancer in an animal: drugs, radiotherapy and surgery.

Owners may delay a veterinary visit if they suspect that something is seriously wrong with their cat, for fear that the vet will suggest euthanasia. But veterinary science has made remarkable strides in recent years and has much to offer. A vet will not suggest euthanasia if there is a reasonable alternative; a vet's goal is to heal and not to kill.

Vets can be as upset by performing euthanasia as the owner permitting it. A survey among vets showed that 41 per cent of female vets and 8 per cent of male vets had cried after euthanising a pet.

An owner should always be alert for the warning signs of illness. Immediate veterinary attention can mean the difference between life and death.

Euthanasia

Attitudes towards pet animals vary enormously. There are those who will present their pets to a vet and ask for it to be euthanised because it made a mess on the carpet or because its colour has changed as it grew up. One survey has shown that 46 per cent of animals are euthanised ('put down' or 'put to sleep') for non-veterinary reasons.

At the other extreme is the owner with a fatally injured or ill pet who pleads with a vet to save their pet no matter what it costs. If the damage is irreparable and the vet is certain that the animal, if it survives any necessary operations, will live in constant pain, euthanasia will be recommended and should be accepted by the owner.

There may never be a time when euthanasia is right but there is a time when prolonging your cat's life is not right. Very few animals die in their sleep.

The Society for Companion Animals Studies suggest the following might be just or humane reasons for euthanasia of a pet:

- Overwhelming physical injuries
- Irreversible disease, to the point that distress or discomfort cannot be controlled

- Old age 'wear and tear' permanently affecting quality of life
- Physical injury, disease or wear and tear causing permanent loss of control of body functions
- Carrying of untreatable disease dangerous to humans
- Aggressiveness with risk to children, owners and others (more likely in a dog than a cat).

SCAS also suggest you ask yourself the following questions:

- Is the condition no longer responsive to treatment?
- Is the pet in physical pain or appearing to be suffering mentally?
- Is the condition prolonged, recurring or getting worse?
- Is it no longer possible to relieve pain?
- If the pet recovers, will it be a chronic invalid?
- Can you provide the necessary care and will this overwhelmingly interfere with your family's life?

If the answer to several of these questions is 'yes', then euthanasia should be discussed with your vet.

Many vets suggest that an owner should not be present while the pet is being euthanised as it will sometimes fight drowsiness to respond to the owner's presence.

Euthanasia is usually carried out by giving a pet a painless injection of an overdose of barbiturates. It is the same type of injection a pet will receive to anaesthetise it for surgery, but in a larger dose. A pet will become drowsy in five seconds, asleep in ten seconds and in cardiac arrest within fifteen seconds. The pet goes quietly to sleep and does not struggle or feel any apprehension. It quietly ceases to be.

Coping with loss

When a much-loved pet dies, grief is necessary to overcome loss and eventually come to terms with it. Yet we live in a culture where we are expected to bear up bravely and not show our feelings. This is particularly true when a pet dies.

'But it was only a cat!' well-meaning friends will exclaim in astonishment at any display of mourning.

Yet that cat has probably spent most of its life with us, giving friendship, companionship and affection. It has shared the bad times with us and helped us rejoice over the good. It has listened to our secrets and passed no judgements. When we have behaved in a way that has been less than fair or honest, it has still loved us uncritically.

It is natural to mourn the passing of a friend. Grief is a necessary part of the recovery process and it passes through several stages.

Numbness
The numb feeling of unreality experienced immediately after the death of any loved one is a safety mechanism. The larger the part played by a pet in an owner's life, the longer this will last. It makes no difference if the pet lived with the owner for a few weeks or for many years; the closer the attachment the owner felt for their cat, the more they will grieve.

Guilt or sorrow
As we begin to acknowledge our loss, sorrow replaces the feeling of numbness. This is the first step in the gradual process of healing. Guilt may arise if a pet has been killed in an accident; we believe the death could have been avoided, and blame ourselves. Guilt can also

begin to overwhelm someone who has had their pet euthanised.

Readjustment

This is the stage where we begin to adjust to life without our pet. We have not forgotten it, but it is at the back of our minds as a pleasant memory, instead of constantly at the forefront. Reaching this stage is more difficult for some than for others; some owners will continue to buy food or toys for their cat long after it has died.

Acceptance

This is the final stage; we accept our pet has gone and the sharp edge of our grief has gone too. There are still times when the pain comes back but we can cope with it. Some owners reach this stage in a few weeks but others will take a year or more to fully accept they will never see their pet again.

Should children be told of the death of a pet? Yes, always. Younger children may accept that their cat has gone to 'heaven' but older children will need more facts. Don't go into any more detail than you have to. I believe it is acceptable to tell children that the pet did not suffer, even if you fear it did. Too much detail can lead to nightmares and if grief is repressed it can resurface in adult life.

Grief therapist Herbert Nieburg, in *Pet Loss* (Herbert A. Nieburg and Arlene Fischer), recognises that repression of grief has an adverse effect on well-being. By not dealing with their feelings, owners allow the pain to remain unrelieved, like an untended sore that never quite heals and interferes with normal functioning.

Grief over the loss of a pet is not only acceptable, it is vitally important.

Should you replace your cat straight away?

It is impossible to replace a cat; you can only acquire another cat.

Each animal is an individual and it is unrealistic to expect any cat to step into the pawprints of another. It won't be able to do so successfully and you will both be disappointed.

For this reason, give yourself some time for the grieving process to work through until you feel capable of treating a new cat or kitten as the individual it is, rather than a replacement for another. Children should be allowed this grieving, and breathing, space too.

All too often, the advice is given, 'Get another cat.' The advice is well-meant and, it has to be said, it sometimes works, although more often it does not. A 'replacement' cat can often be resented, even by the person who has bought it because, by its very presence it reminds them that it is there because a previous, much-loved cat has died.

Cats are not disposable like a product from the supermarket; they are living beings with needs of their own. A cat brought into a grieving household will sense sorrow, and resentment, and will hardly start off its new life well.

Do cats feel grief when a companion cat dies? Without doubt, they do. But, as with humans, there are different degrees of grief. One cat may look for its companion for a few days and then settle down again. Others will grieve for up to six months and may eat very little, stop washing and playing, and hide from their owners.

If this happens, you will have to be patient with your cat and help it work through its grief too. Talk to it, cuddle it and show you care. There may be little reaction to anything you say or do, but one day your cat will start to purr again and you will know the healing process has started.

So remember your other cats when a companion dies; they may be grieving too.

Some cats undergo a remarkable change of personality when a companion cat dies or leaves. A quiet cat which has always been dominated by a stronger personality may come into its own, becoming more lively and playful. A bad-tempered cat may become sunny-natured if the cause of its bad temper has gone. Strangely, a death can lead to a new lease of life for those who remain.

What to do with your cat's body

Macabre as it may seem, the eventual disposal of your cat's body should be considered while your cat is hale, hearty and still with you. When it dies, and especially if death is sudden, you will be too upset to consider what you want to do with your cat's remains. Many owners later wish that they had chosen an option other than the one they did.

Most owners leave their vet to dispose of the body and this is the least expensive option. Disposal of deceased pets is a huge problem for vets and many have to rely on specialist firms to remove sackfuls of pets regularly.

There has been criticism of some of these companies as, in some cases, they have sold the carcases to be processed and sold for fertiliser or other products. There was a scandal in Sweden in the early 1980s when it was discovered that pets' bodies were being turned into pet food. Some pets' bodies end up on council tips and become landfill for new developments.

To overcome these problems, vets who have a sufficiently large practice have installed their own crematoria as have a few charities. Usually, a number of pets are cremated at the same time but, if an owner would like to keep their pet's ashes, their pet can be cremated separately for a slightly higher fee.

Although some owners like to keep their cat's ashes in their homes, others will scatter them at their cat's favourite spot, or will bury them under a decorative tree as a memorial.

Burial is a possibility if you possess a garden. Local bye-laws differ and some authorities will not sanction garden burials. Others will, but will stipulate that the body should be buried at a specified depth, a metre or so. Contact your local town hall for information on this subject.

There are specialist pet cemeteries throughout the world where your pet can be buried alongside others. These cemeteries are usually in peaceful, rural surroundings and are beautifully landscaped. Owners can visit whenever they like and lay flowers on their pet's grave, if they wish. The cemeteries will accept any pet from a budgie to a horse.

Plots can be reserved in advance for a small fee and an annual maintenance agreement ensures the grave will always be well cared for. Burial in a pet cemetery is not a cheap option, but the cost will usually include a simple headstone and a casket, which can range from a simple, polished cabinet to a satin-lined casket with brass handles. Look under 'Cemeteries' in your *Yellow Pages* to find a pet cemetery, or ask your vet if there is one nearby.

In the pet cemetery in Kensington Gardens, London, there is a Victorian cat grave with a headstone carved in Babylonian. The cat was poisoned and the inscription is a Babylonian curse on the perpetrator!

There are other options which pet owners can take advantage of. Some pets' bodies are preserved by taxidermists. If you choose this option, remember that the expertise of taxidermists varies, so, if you have any sporting friends who may have had trophies mounted, ask them to recommend a skilled one. Cats are not easy creatures to preserve in this way and your family pet can end up looking fierce or unnatural. And no taxidermist can replace lost youth or make tired old fur look glossy again.

The latest disposal method comes from the United States. It involves freeze-drying pets, rather like coffee beans, so that their hygienic remains can stay with their owners forever.

Do cats go to heaven?

The possible existence of ghosts has been considered to prove existence of the soul. If this is so, cats must also have souls, as there are many recorded cases of ghost cats.

I know many sane people who have visited friends and commented on their cat (or cats), only to be told that the cat concerned died some time before. Yet these cats can still be seen by their owners, and by other people who did not know of the cats' existence.

When I first moved into my present house, I frequently saw a black cat when I worked in the garden. When I looked for it, it would disappear. Yet there were no black cats living in the area. I enquired into the house's history and discovered a black cat had once lived there many years before. It had had a fairly unpleasant life and was left to have litter after litter of kittens by itself under a nearby railway bridge. When my own cats moved in, the black cat was never seen again. Even ghost cats would seem to recognise others' territory.

Many old buildings have their resident ghost cat. The Borley Rectory in Suffolk, at one time said to be the most haunted house in England, had a ghost cat which terrified the resident moggy so much it became quite neurotic.

The Gateway Restaurant in Battle, Sussex, had a ghost

cat which was seen by owner, staff and guests. When the owner sold the restaurant and moved several miles away, the ghost moggy came with him!

Many owners believe they will be reunited with their pets in the afterlife and many blessing ceremonies are now carried out on pets.

Hosea 2:18 promises: 'And in that day [the day heaven or the new earth is obtained] will I make a covenant for them with the beasts of the field, and with the fowls of heaven and with the creeping things of the ground: . . . and will make them to lie down safely.'

Isaiah 11:6 says: 'The wolf also shall dwell with the lamb, and the leopard shall lie down with the kid; and the calf and the young lion and the fatling together; and a little child shall lead them.'

Perhaps there is room in heaven for our little lions.

Mogastars

Mogs on the box

Could your cat be a television star?
A number of things determine whether or not a cat can be a star of stage and screen – one of them is its colour.

Cats are being used more than ever before in advertising such diverse products as cat food, supermarkets, toilet rolls, banks, sherry and computer software. Most of these cats are moggies who are, according to animal trainers, far better than pedigree cats when it comes to appearing in commercials. Even those television cats which appear to be pedigrees are virtually always half-moggy.

The best moggies for television work are ginger or tabby cats, who not only photograph well but are the easiest cats to train. White cats are also considered to be star material as they are usually placid – but black cats are impossible. According to trainers, they rarely work well and directors are not fond of them either as they are difficult to light!

What sort of cats get into television commercials? They must have a very close relationship with their owners and must have complete faith in them. They should be completely happy in strange surroundings as they will usually have to work in studios. They must be calm when surrounded by strange, and often noisy, people and equipment. In the advertising world, nothing is ever quite ready when it should be and your cat may have to wait while carpenters build sets around it. Your cat may have to work with human models, so should be happy to go to and be held by strangers. One owner of several star moggies insists her cat models are cleverer than their human counterparts – at least they never forget their lines!

Your cat should also be able to follow directions. A director may ask for a cat to walk across a studio along a certain line to a bowl of food, or to lie on a particular chair for some time. If you are able to persuade your cat to follow 'simple' commands such as these, its chance of success is greater. It is also useful if your cat can perform one or two 'tricks' that most cats cannot.

Many cats fail at the audition stage. Usually around a dozen cats are lined up in their carriers. The advertising client will ask for one or two to be taken out for a better look. Often, one of the cats will scoot away – and blows its chances of stardom. A cat which appears nervous or cowed will also be totally unsuitable. It must look happy and totally at home. So you must be as sure as you can be that your cat will be comfortable with the entire process, otherwise there is no point even auditioning.

Your cat should be introduced to travelling, strange places and unfamiliar people from kittenhood, if you would like it to appear in commercials. Trainers often breed their own cats, and start training them at the age of five to six weeks when they are most impressionable.

How to make your cat a star
No cat has ever been serving sodas in a drug store when a producer walks in and offers it a contract.

So you will have to find the breaks for your cat. Scan local and national newspapers carefully, as advertising agencies sometimes appeal for suitable cats in their pages. Advertisements for acting cats appear in papers such as *Stage and Television Today* and occasionally in cat magazines.

For many years, one major pet food manufacturer

found the cats which appeared in its television advertisements (with their owners) through local newspapers throughout the country. Applications were sent to the company's public relations company, so it was not initially clear to the owner that they were applying to appear on television.

For testimonial advertising such as the cat food series, companies ask hopeful owners to send them stories about their cat, including its likes and dislikes. They may also ask for a photograph of cat and owner, so you have to be as photogenic as your cat if you are also to appear in the advertisement. If you are not articulate at the audition (which may be carried out with a video camera in your own home) you blow your cat's chances!

If you are both successfully auditioned (and only six a year out of the thousands who applied are successful for the cat food advertisements) a camera crew may visit your home to make the commercial. This will consist of around twenty people and filming can take several days. Often, equipment will be left in your home overnight so your cat can get used to it and you will be invited to switch on the lights from time to time to accustom your cat to them (and why not – it's your electricity they're using!)

For all this, your cat will earn precisely nothing, because the commercial is a testimonial and the rules say that no financial inducement must be involved. You will be reimbursed for any expenses you have incurred, including any loss of earnings, but your cat will not even receive any free cat food, apart from what it manages to eat while the commercial is being filmed.

Another form of testimonial advertising often used is that which appears in the pet press. So, if there is a product such as flea spray, cat litter, conditioner, or wormers which you think is particularly effective, write to the company and say so in glowing terms, enclosing a good photograph of your cat. The company may simply write back to thank you, but they may use your letter as a testimonial in their adverts and print your cat's photograph too.

Making money

One thing is certain – there's no cat equivalent of Marlon Brando. You won't be able to retire on your cat's earnings.

You may want your cat to appear on television *and* make some money too. There's nothing wrong with that, for you may incur expenses in connection with the appearance (for example, buying a secure cat carrier) and you will certainly be putting in a long day. A cat in a commercial may have to be available at the studio from 8am until as late as midnight.

One way of appearing in paid commercials is to have your cat accepted on the books of an animal model agency or with an animal trainer. The trainers use their own cats when they can so the amount of work from this source might be limited. Look in the *Yellow Pages* locally and in those for your nearest city. From time to time you will see animal trainers interviewed about their work on television and, if that doesn't enable you to track them down, ask the television station for their address or write to them care of the station.

Send them a clear photograph of your cat and tell them why your cat would be good on television. Be sure to mention any particular tricks they can do, such as pushing a doll's pram, or whatever.

Alternatively, write direct to any company which you think might use a cat in its advertising. This doesn't have to be limited to cat food companies or cat equipment manufacturers as so many companies now use cats in commercials. Again, send a clear photo and your cat's *curriculum vitae*.

If you are successful, you will have the satisfaction of knowing that your cat has been seen by millions of people, although it will not necessarily persuade them to buy the product. In a survey I carried out in 1987 among cat owners, 57 per cent said they were *less* likely to buy a product if a cat was used in the advertising.

Unfortunately, you will not get rich. Animals in commercials are paid a straight fee which is hardly generous. And animals never receive residuals!

How to train your cat

Cats *can* be trained. They are not only more intelligent than most other mammals (with the possible exception of humans and apes) but they have good memories and are capable of remembering something shown to them once up to sixteen hours later.

Animal trainers all agree on one point. It is impossible to train an entire cat, so all cat models are neutered.

Cats will only carry out a taught action if there is some advantage for them in doing so. So there must be a reward offered which they receive at no other time. Pet stores sell a variety of cat treats and you should reserve your cat's favourite treats for its training periods.

Place them in a container so that they will make a rattling sound when shaken. First train your cat to come when wanted by rattling the container and rewarding the cat by giving it a treat from the container each time it responds. There is nothing more necessary in any cat owner's life than having a cat which comes to a given signal, yet most owners don't even bother to teach their cats something as simple as this. It is so useful for the times when you want to brush your cat, give it a pill, or just find out where it is. But do give your cat a treat every time it responds to the rattle.

After a few days, when your cat knows and understands this signal, the rest of its training can begin. Choose a time of day when your cat is active, not just after a meal when your cat will want to sleep. If you have a daily playtime with your cat, the training can be incorporated with play. Spend no more than five or ten minutes a day on training as cats lose interest quickly and a bored cat will do nothing.

Cats are required to do a variety of different things in commercials, so train your cat in the simple things. If you can persuade it to sit on command, lie down on command, walk up stairs, look in the direction of a hand signal, or jump from one piece of furniture to another on command, it will already have a wide range of expertise not owned by many other cats. Reward it every time it performs, even if not very well, with a treat and make a fuss of it.

The earlier the training starts the better. If you acquire a young kitten, allow it a few days to settle in and then start training it to come to the rattled treats, graduating to other training in time. Older cats can be trained, but with any cat or kitten, you must be kind, patient and determined.

Help your cat become used to travelling and to other people. Visit friends in their homes taking your cat or kitten with you. If your cat dislikes visiting strange places and hides under a chair, it can never be used on television. If you will be travelling by car to studios, take your cat out in the car frequently, for short trips. If you will be using taxis or trains, you must take your cat out by taxi or train.

If you only take your cat out once a year to receive a vaccination at the vet's, it will be no surprise if your cat becomes nervous when the cat carrier appears!

Cats in contests

Entering contests

Could your moggy be the Tattiest Tomcat, the most Glamorous Granny or the Classiest Cat around?

I ran these contests when I was editor of a cat magazine for there is nothing cat people like better than showing off their cats. One way of achieving fame, if not fortune, for your cat is to enter it in a contest.

All types of magazines and newspapers hold contests for cats and, from time to time, television programmes run contests too. There are a variety of prizes to be won: trophies, cat equipment or, very often, a year's supply of cat food – a valuable prize these days. Most contests are meant to be entertaining and humorous, so bear this in mind when entering. An entertaining and humorous letter is more likely to catch the judges' eyes than one which is seriously factual.

Read, or listen to, the contest rules carefully and, if eligible, follow the rules carefully when entering. Many of these contests ask why your cat should be the winner. Be truthful, but tell the truth amusingly. Don't write down the first reply which comes to mind – several hundred other people will have sent the same reply. Originality is everything.

Spend time working out your answer and try to explain why your cat is really different from other people's cats. Perhaps it understands and obeys forty-two spoken commands, or it saved your life by warning you the house was on fire, or maybe it visits your local hospital and cheers up the patients. Obviously, choose a reason which fits in with the theme of the contest.

Don't apply in verse unless it is really excellent verse. Around half of all cat contest entries are written in (usually very bad) verse. They rarely win.

When you have written down your entry, go over and over it, improving it and polishing it. See if you can write the same phrase in a different, but more entertaining way. Don't tell jokes but be as amusing as possible.

Make sure you enclose your daytime telephone number, even if it's not requested. It's possible you might be shortlisted and contacted by the magazine or newspaper for further information. If they cannot contact you easily, they may go on to the next entrant. And if you are contacted, sound pleased! Nothing is more off-putting than a contestant who sounds as if they don't care whether their cat wins or not.

If the contest is going to run over several issues of the magazine or newspaper, get your entry in right at the beginning. Finalists may appear in each issue and, if your entry is there at the beginning, your cat has a greater chance of becoming a finalist. In the magazine I edited, I printed the contest details one month and showed the first finalist the following month. Because of the length of time it takes to put a magazine together, this left only a few days between the first issue appearing on the bookstalls and the second issue going to press. Anyone who entered within those first few days had very good odds on having their cat chosen because so few entries had been received; whereas at the end of the contest, one or two finalists had to be chosen from hundreds of entries.

These contests usually require a photograph and the better the photo, the better your cat's chances of appearing in print. Newspapers and magazines often send a photographer to take a professional photo if your cat is a finalist or winner, but low-budget magazines will use the photograph you supplied. If it is fuzzy or your cat appears as a tiny blob in one corner, the photo will not be used. If it is a contest to find a beautiful cat, the photograph must show clearly that your cat *is* beautiful.

A self-addressed stamped envelope may be requested for return of your photograph. If so, ensure you send one and that you print your full name and address on the back of the photo. If contest rules state that photographs cannot be returned, *do not* send a SASE and request your photo's return; if you do, the photo will usually be returned without your cat being considered for the contest.

Photographing your cat

When photographing your own cat, you have an advantage over even David Bailey – it's called rapport.

With all animals, and particularly cats, rapport with the subject is probably more important than technical skills and expensive equipment. Of course, technical skills and expensive equipment *help*, so read a few photography manuals to acquire the basic skills and buy the best camera you can afford.

When photographing cats, it is essential to get in really close, so you will need a camera which allows you to get within less than a metre of your subject. A 35 mm Single Lens Reflex (SLR) camera is ideal and you can get a good result with even the most basic model, which will not cost any more than a snapshot camera.

Good photographs are essential if you want to enter your cat in contests, so do not take one or two photographs and use the rest of the film photographing your summer holiday. Do what professional photographers do – take lots of photos. That way, your chances of getting a really good shot are increased.

Buy at least one roll of film to be devoted entirely to your cat photography and use it up within a day or two. Cats move so quickly that the perfect shot has gone by the time you click the shutter. If you take several shots in quick succession, you could get a very pleasant surprise when the film is developed.

If in doubt about lighting or focusing, try the same shot several times at different settings. Don't be afraid to use lots of film – it's relatively cheap. All you need out of a roll of twenty-four or thirty-six exposure film is one good shot. You can then have lots of copies made of that one good shot and use it over and over again. Use a film which will give you prints and negatives and you can have copies made very cheaply. Always use prints when entering contests or sending photographs of your cat to companies which might require cat models, unless slides are specified.

Spend some time working out locations before you bring your cat into the picture. If it has to pose for minutes while you work out camera angles and settings, it will have wandered off, thoroughly bored, by the time you are ready. So find your spot and use a toy or a cushion to stand in for your cat while you work out exactly how you will take the shot.

Does your garden look particularly pretty at a certain time of year? If so, plan your photography for that time using the garden as a backdrop. Remember still to come in really close on your cat, however tempting the background looks.

Backlighting (when the sun is behind your subject) is very effective in cat photography, as the result will be less 'flat'. The fur can appear with a very attractive halo effect, especially if the cat is longhaired. It is a technique which needs experimentation in order to get your settings right. On sophisticated cameras, there is a backlighting button which will automatically give extra exposure to compensate for the fact that the front of your subject is in relative darkness compared to the background. If your camera doesn't have a backlighting button, set your camera manually for around 1½ stops extra exposure. To ensure you get it right, you could take one shot at 1 stop extra exposure, one at 1½ and one at 2 stops extra exposure. One of them should be right!

If you are photographing indoors, plan your background just as carefully. Most cat owners seem to give no thought at all about what is behind their cat because they are so busy concentrating on their pet. Use the toy stand-in while you plan your shot, paying particular attention to the background. You should try to photograph your cat against a plain wall. Fussy wallpapers or carpeting completely overwhelm cat photographs. If you have no suitable plain backgrounds, suspend an ironed, plain sheet or curtaining (not white) behind the cat. This can continue on to the floor where your cat is standing to give a background and foreground of all one colour, such as is used in studio photography.

If you are using flash for indoor shots, beware of red-eye! Cats' eyes often appear red in flash photography using colour film because their retinas are backed by a mirror-like structure which reflects light. When the flash unit is mounted directly on top of the camera, the light reflects straight back at the camera. This can be easily avoided by using a flash unit which is mounted to one side of the camera; only a few centimetres will prevent red-eye. However, the side-mounted flash unit will make your camera rather unstable and you should be careful not to allow your camera to wobble, either by using a tripod, or resting your camera on furniture or a wall.

You can take indoor photographs using available light. On a bright day, pose your cat near the window with the light coming from the side of the camera. This way, you will get light coming across your cat's fur, highlighting it. If you hang a white sheet at the other side of the camera, this will bounce the light back to the other side of the cat.

Don't be afraid to turn your camera through 90 degrees. If your cat is standing side on to you, the standard shot (wider than it is tall) is fine but, if your cat is sitting, it becomes taller than it is wide; turn your camera around so that the photograph is also 'taller'.

Very effective photographs can be taken of just your cat's head; a close-up attachment is necessary for this. If you want your cat to look alert or to look in a particular direction when photographing it, have an assistant attract its attention by rattling a bunch of keys or – a professional photographer's trick – hissing!

If you find you are taking good cat photographs, your cat could appear on a magazine cover or in a calendar. Calendar and greetings cards manufacturers will purchase top-quality cat and kitten photographs. Find their addresses by looking on the cards or calendars or in the *Writers' and Artists' Yearbook*, available at libraries.

Pet magazines are always looking for good cover photographs and will pay for suitable shots. Study the magazine carefully before submitting any photographs as each magazine will have its own style of cover. For example, photographs will almost certainly have to have been taken upright and magazines which enlarge the photograph over the entire cover will require space at the top of the picture over which to print their logo. This space might be as much as one-third of the height of the photograph. Space will also be needed at the sides or bottom of the photograph for the cover lines; the wording which tells you what is in the magazine that week. Send your photographs direct to the magazine editors, with a stamped, self-addressed envelope for their return.

For professional calendars, greetings cards and magazine covers you must use colour transparency (slide) film and you must use a 35 mm or medium or large format camera. Snapshot cameras will not take photographs of the required quality. Film should be 100 ASA or less as the photographs will be enlarged. Faster film than 100 ASA will look too grainy when enlarged.

Show business

Every cat can be a champion

Your cat could be a show champion. It could win prizes worth just as much as a pedigree cat's prizes – which, admittedly, is not a lot!

But no one ever entered a cat in a show for the prizes. We do it because we think our cat is the best in the world and we would like everyone else to have the good fortune to see our cat too. Yet many moggy owners don't realise they can enter their cat in cat shows. Shows are not just for pedigree cats, even when held by pedigree cat clubs. The managers who organise the shows are very keen to have large 'household pet' sections at each show because they believe (rightly) that it is the household pet section which draws the crowds. The crowds, paying an entry fee, make the difference between a show which is a financial success or failure. So don't feel hesitant about entering your moggy in a show if you wish to – you're doing the organisers a favour!

Will your cat enjoy competing in a show? If it doesn't there is no point in showing it. Temperament is important in a show moggy and, if it is not enjoying the show, it will appear miserable. At a show, moggies are not judged on looks; they are judged on personality, charm, health and good grooming.

If your cat is a total extrovert who loves showing off and being admired, and doesn't mind being handled by strangers, it could do very well at a show.

It will spend at least eight hours in a show pen, measuring 60 cm × 60 cm × 60 cm, and only be taken out by white-coated judges who will hold it up to inspect it. All afternoon it will be stared at by spectators who are allowed to look, but not touch, who will ooh and aah over it and say how it looks just like their Sooty/Tiger/Smokey. Some cats adore this; some detest it. You might not find out which type your cat is until after its first show.

In the United Kingdom, there are three organisations under whose rules cat shows are held. These are the Governing Council of the Cat Fancy (GCCF), the longest-established cat registration body; the Cat Association of Britain (CA) and the Independent Pet Cat Society (IPCS), which holds shows only for moggies and 'pet quality' pedigree cats (those which cannot be shown elsewhere).

Shows are usually organised and run by cat clubs under the rules of one of these organisations. The cat clubs may be geographical clubs (for example, the East Sussex Cat Club) where the members have many different breeds of cats but live in the same geographical area. Or they may be breed clubs (for example, the British Ragdoll Club) where the members all share an interest in one breed of cat. Whichever type of club is organising the show, they will welcome moggy competitors, referred to as household pets or pet cats in the show world.

How to enter

It isn't difficult to make your cat a winner if you follow the steps one by one.

First, find your show. You will have to enter at least a month or six weeks before the date of the show, so you must find your show well in advance. If it is the first show for your cat, try to choose one as near your home as possible so that your cat is not upset by travelling a long distance. You can discover when and where shows are to be held from cat magazines or by contacting the organisations under whose rules the shows are held.

Write to the show manager, who organises the event, asking for an entry form (called a schedule). You must enclose a stamped, self-addressed envelope.

Your entry form must be filled in very carefully as any errors may disqualify your cat from competing. Each entry form explains show rules and regulations, abbreviations used and the classes in which you can enter your cat.

Each cat must be entered in an open class and usually, three or four others. The open class for a moggy is its colour. So if you have a three-year-old tabby cat, it would be entered as a 'Tabby or Tabby-and-White Adult'. It can then be entered in three or more miscellaneous classes such as 'Best Groomed Adult or Kitten' or 'Cat with the Prettiest Expression' or 'Cat or Kitten with the Longest Whiskers'. Many of these classes are great fun, giving all sorts of cats a chance to win a rosette. And, if you 'rescued' your cat by acquiring it at a cat shelter, there are classes solely for rescued cats – they're often the prettiest cats at the show!

Fill in the entry form for the number of classes you decide to enter (if it is your cat's first show, restrict it to the minimum number of classes to reduce any stress on your cat). There will be a fee payable for each class entered, which will be slightly reduced if you are a member of the club running the show. You will also have to pay for the pen in which your cat will spend the hours of the show; this is called the benching fee or penning fee. Ensure you enter your cat in the correct classes, bearing in mind its colour, age and sex.

Send the completed form and your fees back to the show manager as soon as possible because, if too many entries are received, only the first entries received will be accepted. Enclose a stamped, self-addressed envelope with your entry, so that you will be sent an acknowledgement that your entry has been received.

Several weeks before the show, you should receive a tally. This is a circular disc with the number of the pen allocated to your cat printed on it. You will also receive a vetting-in card as every cat which enters a show must be checked by the show's vet before being allowed in. Sometimes the tally and vetting-in card will not be posted to you but will be handed to you at the entrance to the show; this should be specified on the schedule you receive.

On the day of the show, take with you the tally and vetting-in card (if they have been sent to you) and your cat's current vaccination certificate against feline enteritis; the vaccination must have been given at least seven days before the show date.

Your cat must be taken to the show in a secure cat-carrying basket or it may be refused entry. You will also need to bring some equipment for your cat's comfort: a tray and litter, drinking and feeding bowls, a blanket and, in the winter, a hot water bottle to place under the blanket. If the show is some distance from your home, you may wish to bottle some tap-water and bring it with you for your cat to drink as water varies in different parts of the country.

You should also bring a comb or brush for a last grooming of your cat before judging and some tissues in case you need to wipe eyes or bottoms!

At GCCF shows, the blanket, tray and bowls must be white and the pen must be undecorated and none of the equipment or the pen must have any distinguishing marks. This is so that judging can be carried out fairly with none of the judges knowing whose cat they are looking at.

At CA and IPCS shows, blanket, tray and bowls can be any colour and the pen can be decorated with curtains and other decorations.

Getting ready

Beauty queens spend months getting ready for a competition — and so do lots of showcats! Preparation enhances the chance of success but I've known many moggy owners at their first show do nothing more than run a comb through their cat's fur half an hour before judging and come away with lots of prizes.

Beauty comes from within and only a really fit and healthy cat will appear at its best. A good diet, supplemented with a conditioner, if necessary, and regular grooming will produce a cat which shows to its best advantage.

Start show grooming several months before the show, if possible. Comb or brush your cat daily and, if you feel it is necessary, give your cat a bath or dry shampoo about a week before the show. (See 'Grooming', p. 165 for further details.) If a dry shampoo is used, or grooming powder, it must be completely brushed out before the show. If any is left in the fur, your cat will be disqualified.

While grooming your cat, check that no fleas or other parasites are present. If they are, deal with them (see 'Moggy Maintenance', p. 159) as your cat will not be allowed into the show hall if it has passengers!

The night before the show, trim your cat's claws (see 'Grooming') and clean its ears, if necessary. Give your cat a good meal and do not allow it outdoors again that night or the next morning. Cat shows start early and, if your cat is not back home in time for you to leave for the show, you will be unable to compete and will forfeit your entry fees.

You will have to be up early on show day as entrants usually have to be at the show hall from 8am to 9am in order to be ready for judging at 10am. Feed your cat, if it is a good traveller, pack all your equipment carefully (a checklist helps) and off you go.

At the top of your checklist you should write 'cat'.

Believe it or not, I have known several people drive to a show only to discover they had brought blankets, bowls, trays, litter, documentation, carriers, brushes, combs, grooming products, cat food, sandwiches, coffee in flasks, tin opener, first aid kits, hot water bottles – but they had forgotten to bring their cat!

What happens at the show

The most nerve-racking part of any show is the vetting-in.

When you arrive at the show, you will have to join a queue for vetting-in. A vet will be on duty to inspect all the cats as they arrive and, if they appear unwell or have any communicable complaint, they will be refused admission. The vet will ask to see an up-to-date certificate of vaccination, so be sure to bring this.

Having passed this hurdle, you find your cat's pen. Each pen is numbered and you should match up the number on your tally with the number on the pen. Before taking your cat out of the carrier, wipe over its pen with disinfectant. These pens have been used by other cats at previous shows and, despite vetting-in, may harbour viruses or germs. Remember that disinfectants based on Phenol or Cresol are poisonous to cats and are not allowed in the show hall.

Place your cat's blanket and litter tray in the pen, tie the tally around its neck using thin white ribbon and give it food and drink to help it settle.

Brush or comb your cat ready for judging and check its ears, eyes and bottom are clean.

At around 10am, judging will begin, and you will have to remove food bowls. At GCCF shows, you will have to leave the hall or stay at the side of the hall until judging is completed about midday. Judges, wearing white coats, will go from pen to pen. A steward will assist them and will push a small trolley, on to which each cat will be lifted for judging. Each exhibit will be returned to its pen and the judge will disinfect his or her hands before passing on to the next cat. (Despite all the precautions, it is possible for your cat to pick up an infection of some kind at a show so it is a good idea to 'quarantine' your showcat for a few days from your other cats when you return home.)

At CA and IPCS shows, the American system of ring judging has been introduced. A steward will bring one cat at a time to the judge who will be stationed at a table, surrounded by chairs occupied by exhibitors and visitors. The judge will inspect the cat publicly, describing the merits of each cat to the spectators. This is a much more interesting way of operating from the spectators' point of view but most cats probably prefer not to be ring-judged as it means they have to be taken from their secure pen and carried through the show hall a number of times.

Winners then have cards detailing their wins attached to their pens. Sometimes, small trophies are given and some pet food companies present winners with cat food. Cats can sometimes win 'specials' too; these are small prizes given by cat club members, usually to cats of their own choice. Specials usually consist of a small gift or trophy. The most usual prize is a rosette, marked with 1st, 2nd or 3rd.

In the afternoon, spectators can walk around and look at cats in their pens. Try to stay near your cat if you can; it will appreciate your company.

No cats are allowed to be taken from the show hall until the show is over, around 5pm to 6pm. So if you have not won anything, you are not allowed to sulk and take your cat home!

Tailpiece

A cat fable

A man loved his cat so much that he decided to name it Heaven.

'Why?' asked his wife.

'Because it is an exceptional cat,' he said. 'It is superior to everything in the world and equal to the heavens.'

'Clouds can hide the heavens,' his wife reminded him.

'I didn't think of that,' he said. 'In that case, I shall call my cat Cloud.'

'Breezes blow away clouds,' his wife commented.

'Then I shall call my cat Breeze.'

'Walls can block a breeze.'

'Then I shall call my cat Wall.'

'Even the smallest mouse can gnaw its way through a wall.'

'Then I shall call my cat Mouse.'

'But even the smallest cat can eat a mouse.'

'You're right! So I shall call my cat, Cat.'

His wife smiled. 'A cat can never be anything *but* a cat,' she said.

INDEX